Machine Knits

MACHINE Knits

Valerie Carter

Bell & Hyman

Published in 1986 by
Bell & Hyman Limited
Denmark House
37–39 Queen Elizabeth Street
London SE1 2QB

British Library Cataloguing in Publication Data

Carter, Valerie
    Machine knits.
    1. Knitting, Machine
    2. Knitting Patterns
    I. Title
746.43'2041   TT687

ISBN 0 7135 2663 7

Designed by Janet Tanner
Diagrams by Ken Kitchen
Photographs by Helen Pask
Typeset by Tradespools Ltd, Frome
Colour separation by Positive Colour Ltd, Maldon
Printed in Great Britain by Scotprint Ltd, Musselburgh

Yarn Suppliers

All the yarns used throughout this
book are freely available from
knitting machine and wool shops
in the United Kingdom and were
kindly supplied by the following
companies.

ARGYLL WOOLS LTD
PO BOX 15
PRIESTLEY MILLS
PUDSEY
WEST YORKSHIRE
LS28 9LT

BRAMWELL & CO LTD
HOLMES MILL
GREENACRE STREET
CLITHEROE
LANCS

BSK LTD
MURDOCK ROAD
MANTON INDUSTRIAL ESTATE
BEDFORD
MK41 7NE

ROWAN YARNS
COLOURWAY
112A WESTBOURNE GROVE
LONDON
W2 3RU

If you have any difficulty in
finding the yarns you require, a
mail order service is available
from both Bramwell Ltd and BSK
Ltd.

INTRODUCTION

This book is not intended to teach you to machine knit, there can be no substitute for the instruction book that is supplied with the machine.

It is a book packed full of wearable fashion knitwear that can be worn all year round and contains a guide to the basic techniques which have been used to knit and finish the patterns.

There are many makes and models of knitting machines on the market and these patterns are suitable for the most popular leading brands of punchcard knitting machines which are available today.

PUNCHCARDS

When knitting a punchcard design from this book, you must make sure that the card is punched so that row one is at the correct starting point for your machine. Row one must be programmed into the machine before the pattern can be knitted.

Some Toyota machines knit the card in reverse so either the yarns need to be changed round or the card punched in reverse.

If the cards are punched out correctly they will work on almost any automatic 24 stitch pattern repeat punchcard knitting machine.

TENSION

These patterns were all knitted on either a 'Jones+Brother', 'Knitmaster' or 'Toyota' punchcard knitting machine. Every machine may vary a little, so all tensions given are only approximate.

Using the correct yarn and tension will not always result in the garment being the correct size, a 4-ply Acrylic in a dark colour will knit up much tighter than a pale colour of the same yarn.

To achieve perfect results it is important to knit a test swatch. The tension dial on the carriage has whole numbers with dots in between the numbers. With some machines it may be necessary to adjust the dial by only one dot, others may vary as much as two or three whole numbers. The only way you can guarantee to achieve the correct tension is to knit a tension swatch, which can be stored for future reference.

KNIT A TEST SWATCH AS FOLLOWS:

If the pattern says MATERIAL: 4-ply
TENSION: 32 sts × 44 rs = 10cm (4 in)
T at approx 6

You will need two shades of the 4-ply you are going to knit the garment in. Colour 1, Main Yarn (MY) and colour 2, Waste Yarn (WY).

Cast on more than 70 sts in WY, leaving the 17th stitch each side of centre 0 in Non Working Position (NWP).
* Tension dial (T) at 6.
Knit a few rows in WY.
Change to MY, Knit 44 rs.
Change to WY, Knit 6 rs. *

Repeat from * to * moving the tension dial up or down as required.

Leave the swatch overnight, or for several hours to return to its natural shape. Press the swatch the same way as given in the final making up instructions of the pattern being knitted. Measure the swatch between the ladder created by the missing stitch, to give the number of stitches. It should measure 10cm (4in). Then measure the distance between the colour changes—that should measure 10cm (4in) also.

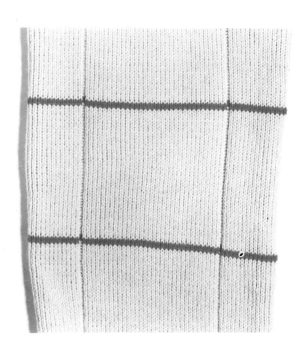

TECHNIQUES

Cast on in Waste Yarn (WY)

This type of cast on is used when hems are being worked or when the ribs or welts are being added later.

WY is yarn that is going to be removed from the main knitting, so it can be different from the yarn used to knit the garment. This is a good way of using up some of those odd yarns, although it is easier to handle if the WY is the same weight as the Main Yarn (MY).

Push forward the required number of needles into Working Position (WP). Thread the carriage with WY. Knit several rows ending with the carriage on the left.

Thread up the nylon cord and knit one row. This separates the waste knitting from the main knitting. (There are several different colours available in nylon ravel cords, so use one of a contrasting colour to make separation easier.)

Change to MY and continue to knit pattern.

WY should not be removed until the garment is finished.

Cast on by hand

This gives a closed edge cast on. It may also be known as 'cast on by hand using the e method'.

Starting with the carriage at the right and with the yarn on the left, bring forward the required number of needles into Holding Position (HP). Secure the yarn with a slip knot around the first needle on the left.

Wind the yarn round each needle in an anti-clockwise direction, as if you were making a letter 'e' over each needle. Try not to pull the yarn too tight and to keep the loops even.

When all the needles are wrapped, thread the yarn through the carriage ready to knit. Take up any slack yarn.

With the carriage set to knit back the needles, knit one row.* Push all needles back into HP, knit one row*, repeat from * to * until enough knitting has been produced to enable small claw weights to be hung. Then continue to knit as normal.

When the carriage and yarn are at the left and the pattern says c.on by hand xx number of stitches at the left, unthread the yarn from the carriage, pull the required number of needles into HP and work the c.on in reverse starting at the right and winding the yarn in a clockwise direction, finishing at the left. Re-thread the yarn and work as before.

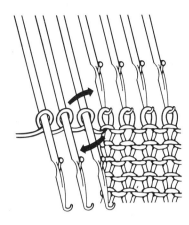

Ribs and Welts

The instructions for the patterns in this book are given for machines with ribbing attachments. For machines without a ribber, the ribs and welts can be worked either in continental rib or by reforming the stitches.

Continental rib

Cast on in WY, 1 × 1, the number of stitches stated in the pattern. Knit a few rows ending with the carriage at the left, knit one row with the nylon cord.

With the MY, and with the tension dial at least three numbers lower than the main tension, work approximately two thirds the number of rows stated in the pattern: i.e. if the pattern says K 30 rows, knit 20 rows for continental rib, knit one row at a large tension—for the folding line—then work the same number of rows at the previous tension.

Turn up hem.

Reformed ribs

Cast on in WY, 1 × 1, the number of stitches stated in the pattern. Leave two needles at the left in WP.

Knit a few rows, ending with the carriage at the left. Knit one row with the nylon cord. Thread the carriage with the MY. With the tension dial at 0, knit four rows.

Insert the transfer tool into the loop of the first row of main knitting, and place it onto the first needle at the left.

Bring forward the empty needles into WP. With the tension dial one tension tighter than the main knitting, knit the required number of rib rows.

Working from the third needle at the left, insert the latch tool/tappet under the first row of the main knitting and reform the stitch with the latch tool.

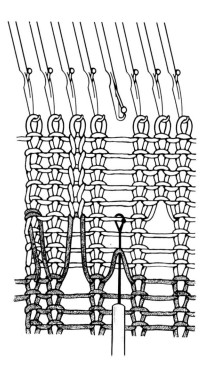

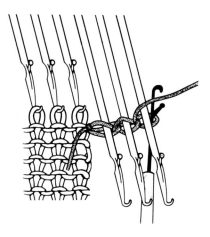

Bring the same needles into holding position before knitting the next few rows.

Working with nylon cord

Use nylon cord when knitting a shaped neck and the pattern says knit back on nylon cord.

Bring the required number of needles into holding position and lay the nylon cord across them, making sure that the cord is in front of the latches.

Manually knit one needle at a time back into non working position.

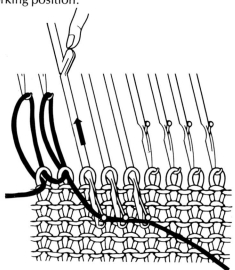

To replace the stitches onto the needles, with both hands pull both ends of the cord.

When all the needles are in working position hold one end of the cord and pull the other end upwards to unravel the stitches.

Cast off with latch tool

Before working cast off row *always* knit one row at the largest tension possible. When working with fine yarns, knit one row with the tension 3 or 4 numbers higher than the main knitting.

Bring all needles into holding position. On the side opposite to the carriage, hook the latch tool into the first stitch and push the stitch behind the latch. Hook the tool into the second stitch leaving this

Shaping

When knitting fairisle or stitch patterns, it is not necessary to work fully fashioned shapings. On stocking stitch garments, though, fully fashioned shapings look more professional.

Fully fashioned decrease

This can be worked as many stitches into the work as may be required, but is normally worked two or three needles in.

With a two or three pronged tool, transfer the end stitches onto adjacent needles, leaving the end one empty—push this back to NWP.

Fully fashioned increase

This can also be worked as many stitches into the work as may be required, but is similarly normally worked two or three stitches in.

Bring forward to working position one needle. Working with a two or three pronged tool, transfer the end stitches to the outside.

With a single end tool, pick up the loop from the third or fourth stitch and place it onto the empty needle.

Multiple stitch increase

When a pattern calls for more than two stitches to be increased at the left or right, use the closed edge cast on method as shown in the cast on by hand section, or use the chain method.

On the opposite side to the carriage bring forward into holding position the number of needles required. Using a spare piece of MY and the latch tool/tappet, work a chain stitch over each needle, working from the edge of the work to the outside.

stitch in the hook. Bring the latch tool forward drawing the first stitch over the second.

Push the second stitch behind the latch. Hook the latch tool into the third stitch and repeat as before.

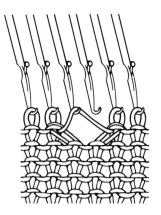

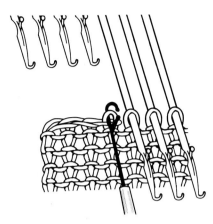

Then pick up the loop previously removed and place it onto the needle above where the bar was picked up from. Continue to knit.

To finish off pull the yarn through the last stitch with the latch tool.

Buttonholes

Small buttonholes are worked by transferring one stitch onto an adjacent needle, leaving the empty needle in working position.

This method works just as well when working on a single bed or double bed machine. When working with a double bed machine transfer the stitch from the front bed to the adjacent needle on the main bed—leaving the empty needle in working position.

Medium buttonholes

These are worked over two needles by transferring two stitches onto their respective adjacent needles leaving the empty needles in working position, then knitting one row.

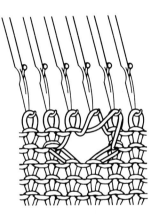

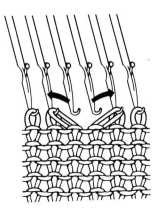

Remove the loop from the right stitch and pick up the bar beneath the stitch to the right. Knit one row.

Large buttonholes

These are worked over three or more stitches for any size of button.

Have a piece of MY ready to cast on the stitches at the top of the buttonhole.

Transfer one stitch onto the adjacent needle to the right and then transfer these two stitches onto the empty needle.

Bring the needle forward until the stitch at the back passes over the latch hook. Take the needle back, drawing the back stitch over the front one.

Continue to work, repeating all the above over the number of stitches required.

Place the last stitch onto the next needle on the left.

For the upper edge, cast on with MY using the chain method. Bring all the needles used for the buttonhole into holding position before knitting the next few rows.

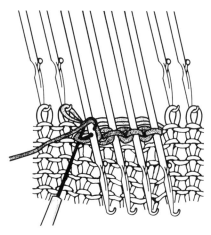

Finishing

Try to press knitwear on a large flat surface. First pin out each piece of knitting with the wrong side facing you, carefully checking the size.

After reading the manufacturer's or pattern instructions, press the knitting with a smooth action. Do not wet press unless stated in the pattern.

Backstitch

After letting the knitting cool from pressing, pin the pieces together. For the sleeve and side seams, backstitch gives a very simple, firm seam. Using a wool needle with a rounded point, join the seam by working small running stitches which overlap.

Mattress stitch

For a really professional finish, mattress stitch is the neatest stitch for sewing up knitwear. It can, however, be more difficult as it is worked on the right side of the garment. Working with the right side of the garment in view does make matching stripes and patterns much easier.

Join the yarn to the fabric, insert the needle into two bars of the knitting, one complete stitch in. Then take the needle across to the other piece and pick up the two corresponding bars.

Repeat this, working down the seam, it is not necessary to keep pulling the yarn, several stitches can be worked before pulling the yarn to join the seam.

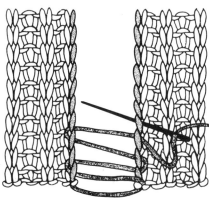

Grafting

When there are two open edges of the same length to be joined, graft stitch can be worked to produce a joining row which looks as if it has been knitted.

After pressing the pieces, working with a round ended needle threaded with the same yarn as the garment, lay the pieces together with the right sides facing.

Insert the needle from the back into the first stitch of the lower piece of knitting (1). Next, insert the needle from the back into the first stitch of the upper piece (2).

Insert the needle from the front, into the first stitch of the lower piece and into the back of the next stitch (3). Insert the needle from the front into the first stitch of the upper piece and into the back of the next stitch (4).

Continue to work the seam until all the loops are joined. Do not pull the yarn too tight.

Crochet edge

To trim the edge of neckline bands and hems with crochet stitch, join the yarn to the knitting with a crochet hook.

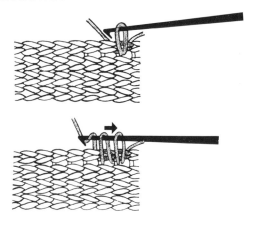

Work along the edge as shown.

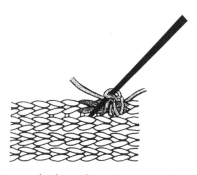

Continue to work along the edge, repeating these steps. At appropriate intervals, miss out a stitch from the knitting to form a firm edge.

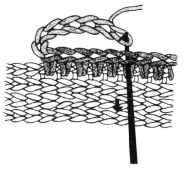

Continue to work in crochet stitch along the edge of the knitted fabric until the next buttonhole is required.

Crochet button loop

Working with a crochet hook, work crochet stitches as shown for making a crochet edge along the edge of the knitted fabric, up to the point where a buttonhole needs to be worked. Then crochet a chain to form a loop big enough to fit the size of button required. Remove the hook from the last chain stitch and insert it into crochet stitch.

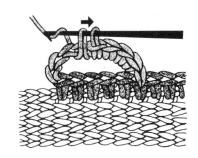

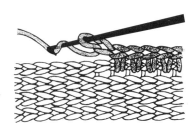

Pick up the last chain stitch and pull it through the crochet stitch. Then work crochet stitches along the chain stitches, working at least three more stitches than those worked in chain stitch.

ABBREVIATIONS							

alt	Alternate	in	Inch/es	r/s	Row/s
approx	Approximate	inc	Increase	rel	Release
beg	Beginning	K	Knit	rem	Remaining
carr	Carriage	mach	Machine	rep	Repeat
cm	Centimetre/s	M/bed	Main bed	rev	Reversing
cent	Centre	MT	Main Tension	st/s	Stitch/es
c.on	Cast on	MT−1	Main Tension − 1	SS	Stocking Stitch
c.off	Cast off	MT+1	Main Tension + 1	T	Tension dial
col(s)	Colour(s)	MY	Main Yarn	trans	Transfer
cont	Continue	n/s	Needle/s	WY	Waste Yarn
dec	Decrease	NWP	Non Working Position	WP	Working Position
ev	Every	oppos	Opposite		
FF	Fully Fashioned	patt	Pattern	*Note:*	Rib Tensions
foll	Following	pos	Position	T1/1	Tension 1 on both beds.
HP	Holding Position	RC	Row Counter	T10/8	Tension 10 on main bed
					Tension 8 on ribber bed.

Numbers cardigan.

Sizes 56 (61,66)cm (22 (24, 26)in)

Materials 1 cone each BK
Charisma cols A & B
7 buttons
card 1

Tension 32 sts × 35 rs = 10cm
(4in) over patt
T at approx 7

BACK
Insert card & lock to K row 1.
Col A, c.on in 1 × 1 rib 95 (103, 111) sts.
RC 000, T3/3, K 16 rs.
Trans sts to M/bed.
RC 000, MT, working in fairisle, K 66 rs.

Shape armholes
C.off 4 sts beg next 2 rs.
Dec 1 st both ends next & foll 4th rs.
12 times in all.
Cont to K until RC 114 (120, 126) rs.
C.off.

RIGHT FRONT
Insert card & lock to K row 1.
Counting from 2nd (4th, 4th) ns left cent 0.
Col A, c.on in 1 × 1 rib 45 (49, 53) sts.
RC 000, T3/3, K 16 rs.
Trans sts to M/bed.
RC 000, MT, working in fairisle, K 66 rs.

Shape armhole
C.off 4 sts beg next r, K 1 r.
Dec 1 st at armhole next & foll 4th rs.
12 times in all.

At same time
on r 97 (1 r extra for left front):

Shape neck
C.off 7 sts beg next r.
Dec 1 st at neck next & foll alt rs.
12 times in all.
Cont to K until RC 114 (120, 126) rs.
C.off.

LEFT FRONT
Rep as for right front, rev all shaping.

SLEEVES
Insert card & lock to K row 1.
Col A, c.on in 1 × 1 rib 45 (51, 57) sts.
RC 000, T2/2, K 16 rs.
Trans sts to M/bed.
RC 000, MT, working in fairisle, K 4 rs.

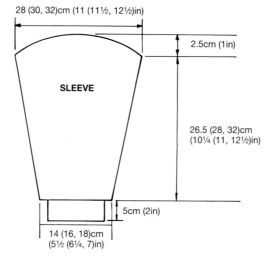

28 (30, 32)cm (11 (11½, 12½)in)

2.5cm (1in)

SLEEVE

26.5 (28, 32)cm (10¼ (11, 12½)in)

5cm (2in)

14 (16, 18)cm (5½ (6¼, 7)in)

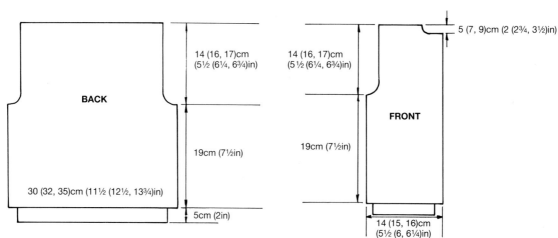

14 (16, 17)cm (5½ (6¼, 6¾)in)

14 (16, 17)cm (5½ (6¼, 6¾)in)

5 (7, 9)cm (2 (2¾, 3½)in)

BACK

FRONT

19cm (7½in)

19cm (7½in)

30 (32, 35)cm (11½ (12½, 13¾)in)

5cm (2in)

14 (15, 16)cm (5½ (6, 6¼)in)

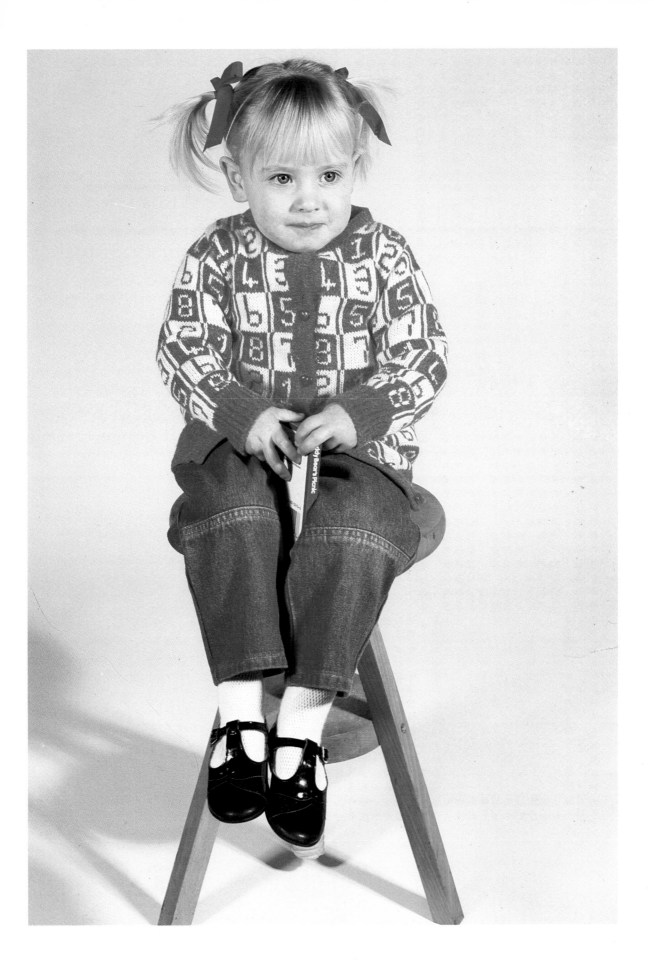

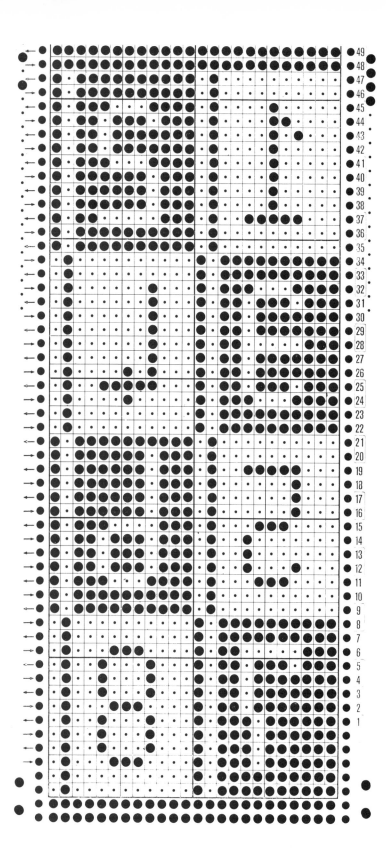

Inc 1 st both ends next & foll 4th rs until 89 (95, 101) sts.
Cont to K until RC 92 (98, 102) rs.
C.off 10 sts beg next 8 rs.
C.off rem sts.
Join shoulder seams.

NECKBAND
Bring forward 81 (87, 93) ns.
With wrong side facing, pick up sts evenly around neck.
T7, K 1 r. T5, K 3 rs. T3, K 3 rs.
T9, K 1 r. T3, K 3 rs. T5, K 3 rs.
T7, K 1 r. Rel work on WY.

BUTTONHOLE BAND
Bring forward 101 (107, 113) ns.
With wrong side facing, pick up sts evenly along front edge.
T3, K 6 rs.
Work 7 buttonholes evenly along next r.
T3, K 6 rs. T9, K 1 r. T3, K 6 rs.
Work 7 buttonholes over last set.
T3, K 6 rs.
Rel work on WY.

BUTTONBAND
K as for buttonhole band omitting buttonholes.

TO MAKE UP
Insert sleeves, sew side & sleeve seams.
Fold all bands to inside & back st through open loops into pos.
Sew on buttons.
Press lightly with cool iron.

Alphabet sweater.

(See photograph on page 16)

Sizes 61 (66, 71)cm (24 (26, 28)in)

Materials 1 cone each BK Charisma cols A & B card 2

Tension 31 sts × 36 rs = 10cm (4in) over patt T at approx 7

BACK & FRONT ALIKE
(K two)
Insert card & lock to K row 1.
Col A, c.on in 1 × 1 rib 101 (109, 117) sts.
RC 000, T3/3, K 16 rs.
Trans sts to M/bed.
RC 000, MT, working in fairisle, K 70 (76, 82) rs.

Shape armholes
C.off 4 sts beg next 2 rs.
Cont to K until RC 127 (134, 140) rs.
Trans sts to 1 × 1 rib.
Col A, T3/3, K 10 rs. T10/8, K 1 r.
T3/3, K 10 rs. T10/8, K 1 r.
C.off loosely.

SLEEVES
Insert card & lock to K row 1.
Col. A, c.on in 1 × 1 rib 49 (55, 61) sts.
RC 000, T3/3, K 16 rs.
Trans sts to M/bed.
RC 000, MT, working in fairisle, inc 1 st both ends next & foll 4th rs until 91 (97, 103) sts.
Cont to K until RC 90 (96, 100) rs.

Shape top
C.off 10 sts beg next 8 rs.
C.off rem sts.

TO MAKE UP
Fold bands to inside and slip st into pos.
Join shoulder 7cm (2¾in) each side.
Insert sleeves, sew side and sleeve seams.
Press very lightly with cool iron.

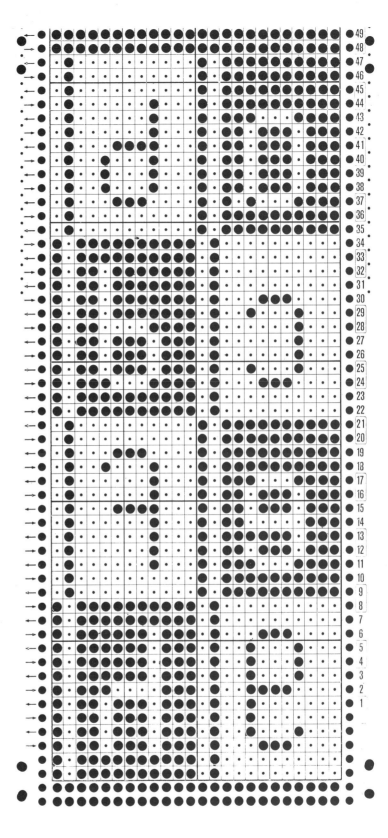

Alphabet sweater—see pattern on page 15

Dungaree set—see pattern on page 18

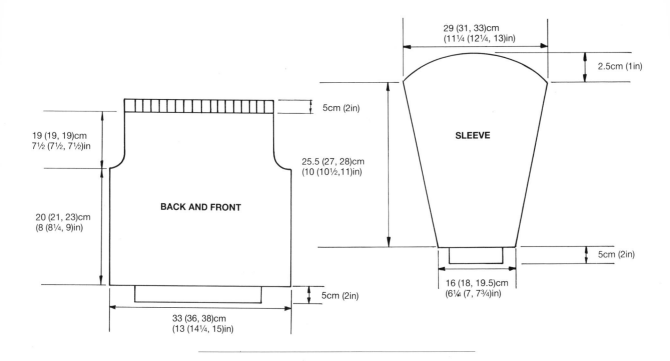

29 (31, 33)cm
(11¼ (12¼, 13)in)

2.5cm (1in)

SLEEVE

5cm (2in)

19 (19, 19)cm
7½ (7½, 7½)in

25.5 (27, 28)cm
(10 (10½,11)in)

BACK AND FRONT

20 (21, 23)cm
(8 (8¼, 9)in)

5cm (2in)

16 (18, 19.5)cm
(6¼ (7, 7¾)in)

5cm (2in)

33 (36, 38)cm
(13 (14¼, 15)in)

![Dungaree set.]

(See photograph on page 17)

(Knitted all in one piece)

Sizes 46 (51, 56, 61)cm (18 (20, 22, 24)in)

Materials 1 cone BK 4-ply Acrylic col A
Small amount of col B
2 press studs
3 buttons
Knit-in-Elastic
card 3

Tension 28 sts × 40 rs = 10cm (4in)
T at approx 6

Dungarees

FIRST LEG

Counting from 5th n from left cent to left, c.on in WY 63 (67, 71, 75) sts.

K few rs.
Carr at left.
K 1 r in nylon cord.
Col A, RC 000, MT, K 81 (87, 93, 99) rs.
C.on 3 sts by hand, beg next r.
Carr at right.
Break yarn, place all sts into HP or K back onto nylon cord.

SECOND LEG

Counting from 4th n, right cent to right, c.on in WY 63 (67, 71, 75) sts.
K few rs.
Carr at left.
K 1 r in nylon cord.
Col A, RC 000, MT, K 81 (87, 93, 99) rs.
Carr at left.
C.on 7 sts by hand, beg next r.
RC 82 (88, 94, 100).

BODY

Bring all ns at left back into WP.
C.on 3 sts by hand, beg next r.
RC 000, K 74 (82, 90, 98) rs.
Trans sts to 1 × 1 rib.
Weight work.
Working with col A & Knit-in-Elastic, both in feeder 1, T1/1, K 8 (8, 10, 10) rs.
C.off 53 (55, 57, 59) sts beg next 2 rs.
Trans sts to M/bed.
Remove Knit-in-Elastic.

BIB

Insert card & lock to K row 1.

Work on cent 33 (37, 41, 45) sts.
Col A, RC 000, MT, K 4 (6, 8, 10) rs.
Rel card & work motif.
Cont to K until RC 28 (32, 36, 40) rs.
Rel work on WY.

ANKLES

Col A, c.on in 1 × 1 rib 41 (43, 45, 47) sts.
RC 000, T1/1, K 3 (3, 3, 5) rs.
Col B, K 6 rs.
Col A, K 3 (3, 3, 5) rs.
Trans sts to M/bed.
With wrong side facing, pick up sts evenly around ankle.
MT, K 1 r. T10, K 1 r.
C.off with latch tool.

BIB-BAND
Sides

(K two)
Col A, c.on in 1 × 1 rib 25 (27, 29, 31) sts.
RC 000, T2/2, K 1 r.
Dec 1 st at right next 6 rs.
K 1 r.
Trans sts to M/bed.
With wrong side facing & with dec edge to top, pick up sts evenly down side of bib.
MT, K 1 r. T10, K 1 r.
C.off with latch tool.
Work second side, rev. shaping.

Top

Col A, c.on in 1 × 1 rib 41 (45, 49, 53) sts.

RC 000, T2/2, K 1 r.
Dec 1 st both ends next 6 rs.
K 1 r.
Trans sts to M/bed.
With wrong side facing pick up
sts held on WY.
MT, K 1 r. T10, K 1 r.
C.off with latch tool.

STRAPS
Col A, c.on in 1 × 1 rib 13 (13,
13, 15) sts.
RC 000, T2/2, K 92 (98, 108,
118) rs.
C.off.

TO MAKE UP
Sew leg & back seams.
Join bib bands, sew straps to back
waist & attach press studs to front.
Press with cool iron.

Sweater

BACK
Col A, c.on in 1 × 1 rib 67 (75,
83, 91) sts.
RC 000, T1/1, K 5 rs.
Col B, K 6 rs.
Col A, K 5 rs.
Trans sts to M/bed.
Inc 1 st.
RC 000, MT, K 56 (66, 66, 76) rs.

Shape raglan
C.off 4 sts beg next 2 rs.
Dec 1 st both ends next & foll 4th
rs.
3 times in all.
K 1 r.
Dec 1 st, both ends next & foll
alt rs until 26 (28, 30, 32) sts rem.
Rel work on WY.

FRONT
K as for back until RC 86 (96,
108, 118).

Shape neck
C.off cent 14 (16, 18, 18) sts.
Place all sts left cent into HP.
Keeping raglan shaping correct,
Dec 1 st at neck next 3 rs.
Dec 1 st at neck next & foll alt rs 2
(2, 2, 3) times in all.
Cont to dec at raglan until all sts
have been dec.
Complete left side rev shaping.

SLEEVES
Col A, c.on in 1 × 1 rib 33 (37,
41, 45) sts.
RC 000, T1/1, K 5 rs.
Col B, K 6 rs.
Col A, K 5 rs.
Trans sts to M/bed.

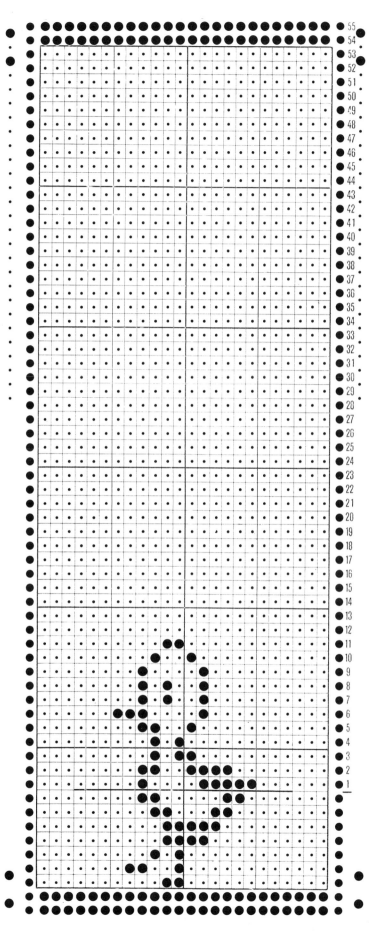

Inc 1 st.
RC 000, MT, K 2 rs.
Inc. 1 st both ends next & foll 6th rs until 48 (54, 60, 66) sts.
Cont to K until RC 62 (62, 62, 72).

Shape top

C.off 3 sts beg next 2 rs.
Dec 1 st both ends next & foll 4th rs.
3 times in all.
K 1 r.
Dec 1 st both ends next & foll alt rs until 6 sts rem.
Rel work on WY.

NECKBAND

Col A, c.on in 1 × 1 rib 69 (75, 81, 87) sts.
RC 000, T1/1, K 3 rs.
T2/2, col B, K 4 rs.
T3/3, col A, K 3 rs.
Trans sts to M/bed.
With wrong side facing, pick up sts held on WY at back, sleeve, down front shaping, across sts held on WY, up front shaping, & sts held on WY on sleeve.
MT, K 1 r. T10, K 1 r.
C.off with latch tool.

TO MAKE UP

Sew left raglan & right raglan from armhole to 7.5cm (3in) from top.
Sew side & sleeve seams.
Work 1 r crochet slip st, & 2 rs double crochet along back & front sleeve opening, working 3 button holes on front.
Sew buttons to back.
Press with warm iron.

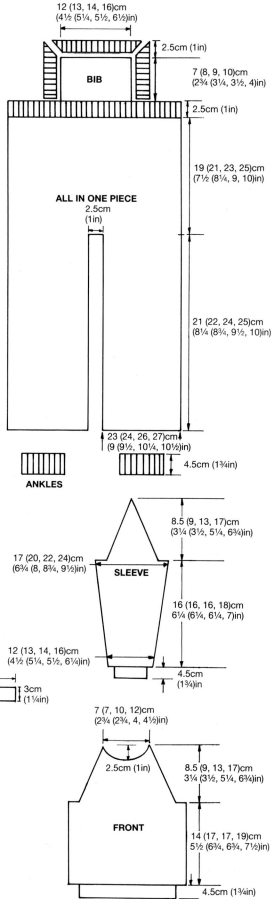

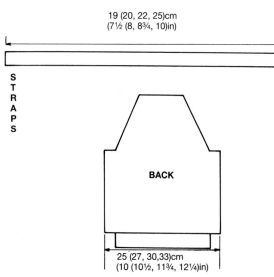

Dress—see pattern on page 22

Dress.

(See photograph on page 21)

Sizes 41 (46, 51, 56, 61)cm (16 (18, 20, 22, 24)in)

Materials 1 cone BK Charisma
4 buttons
lace
ribbon

Tension 32 sts × 42 rs = 10cm (4in)
T at approx 7

FRONT

C.on in 1 × 1 rib 131 (143, 159, 175, 191) sts.
RC 000, T2/2, K 6 rs.
Trans sts to M/bed.
Inc. 1 st, RC 000, MT, K 2 rs.
** Trans ev other st onto adjacent ns.
Leaving empty ns in WP, K 4 rs.**
Rep from ** to ** two more times.
Cont to K until RC 76 (80, 86, 92, 98).
Rel work on WY.

BODICE

Bring forward 66 (72, 80, 88, 96) ns.
With wrong side facing, pick up sts from skirt placing 2 sts on each n.
RC 000, MT, K 2 rs.
Counting from 2nd n from right trans ev 4th st onto adjacent ns.
Leaving empty ns in WP, K until RC 10 (14, 22, 30, 38).*

Shape armholes

RC 000, c.off 5 (6,7,7,8) sts beg next 2 rs.
Dec 1 st both ends next & foll alt rs until 50 (56, 62, 68, 74) sts rem.
K 0 (4, 8, 10, 14) rs.
** Trans ev other st onto adjacent ns.
Leaving empty ns in WP, K 4 rs.**
Rep from ** to ** once.
Trans ev other st onto adjacent ns.
Leaving empty ns in WP, K 2 rs.
RC 18 (20, 24, 28, 32).

Shape neck

C.off cent 12 (12, 14, 14, 16) sts.
Place all sts left cent into HP or K back onto nylon cord.

At neck edge

Dec 1 st next & foll alt rs, 6 (7, 8, 10, 11) times in all.
Cont to K until RC 44 (50, 56, 62, 68).

Shape shoulder

C.off 4 (5, 5, 5, 6) sts beg next r.
K 1 r.
C.off 4 (5, 5, 6, 6) sts beg next r.
K 1 r.
C.off 5 (5, 6, 6, 6) sts beg next r.
Complete left side, rev shaping.

BACK

K as for front to *.

Shape armholes

RC 000, C.off 5 (6, 7, 7, 8) sts beg next 2 rs.

Divide for back opening

With spare piece of MY, c.off cent 4 sts.
Place all sts left cent into HP or K back onto nylon cord.
Dec 1 st at armhole edge next & foll alt rs until 23 (25, 29, 32, 35) sts rem.
Cont to K until RC 44 (50, 56, 62, 68).

Shape shoulder

C.off 4 (5, 5, 5, 6) sts beg next r.

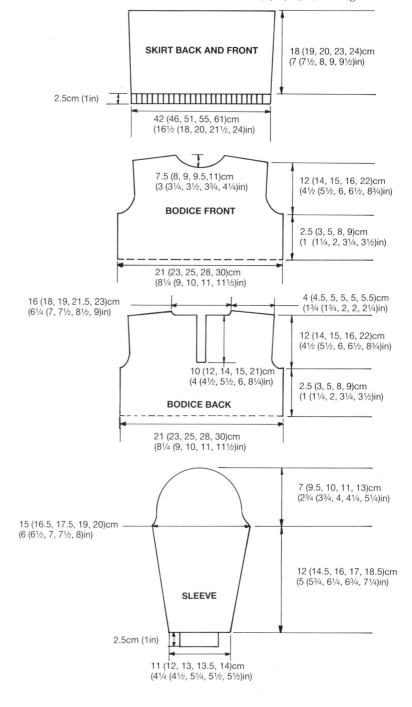

SKIRT BACK AND FRONT

18 (19, 20, 23, 24)cm (7 (7½, 8, 9, 9½)in)

2.5cm (1in)

42 (46, 51, 55, 61)cm (16½ (18, 20, 21½, 24)in)

BODICE FRONT

7.5 (8, 9, 9.5,11)cm (3 (3¼, 3½, 3¾, 4¼)in)

12 (14, 15, 16, 22)cm (4½ (5½, 6, 6½, 8¾)in)

2.5 (3, 5, 8, 9)cm (1 (1¼, 2, 3¼, 3½)in)

21 (23, 25, 28, 30)cm (8¼ (9, 10, 11, 11½)in)

BODICE BACK

16 (18, 19, 21.5, 23)cm (6¼ (7, 7½, 8½, 9)in)

4 (4.5, 5, 5, 5.5)cm (1¾ (1¾, 2, 2, 2¼)in)

12 (14, 15, 16, 22)cm (4½ (5½, 6, 6½, 8¾)in)

10 (12, 14, 15, 21)cm (4 (4½, 5½, 6, 8¼)in)

2.5 (3, 5, 8, 9)cm (1 (1¼, 2, 3¼, 3½)in)

21 (23, 25, 28, 30)cm (8¼ (9, 10, 11, 11½)in)

SLEEVE

7 (9.5, 10, 11, 13)cm (2¾ (3¾, 4, 4¼, 5¼)in)

15 (16.5, 17.5, 19, 20)cm (6 (6½, 7, 7½, 8)in)

12 (14.5, 16, 17, 18.5)cm (5 (5¾, 6¼, 6¾, 7¼)in)

2.5cm (1in)

11 (12, 13, 13.5, 14)cm (4¼ (4½, 5¼, 5½, 5½)in)

At neck edge
C.off 10 (10, 13, 15, 17) sts beg next r.
C.off 4 (5, 5, 6, 6) sts beg next r.
K 1 r.
C.off rem sts.
Complete left side, rev shaping.

SLEEVES
C.on in 1 × 1 rib 35 (37, 41, 43, 45) sts.
RC 000, T1/1, K 16 rs.
Trans sts to M/bed.
Inc 1 st, RC 000, MT, K 4 rs.
Inc 1 st, both ends next & foll 6th rs until 48 (52, 56, 60, 64) sts.
Cont. to K until RC 50 (60, 66, 72, 78).

Shape top
C.off 3 sts beg next 2 rs.
Dec 1 st both ends next & foll alt rs 11 (15, 17, 20, 23) times.

Dec 1 st both ends next 6 rs.
C.off rem sts.
Join shoulder seams.

NECKBAND
C.on in 1 × 1 rib 69 (75, 81, 87, 95) sts.
RC 000, T2/3, K 6 rs.
Trans sts to M/bed.
With wrong side facing, pick up sts from around neck, starting from back opening.
MT, K 1 r. T10, K 1 r.
C.off with latch tool.

BUTTONBAND
C.on in 1 × 1 rib 35 (37, 39, 43, 47) sts.
RC 000, T2/3, K 6 rs.
Trans sts to M/bed.
With wrong side facing, pick up sts evenly along right opening.

MT, K 1 r. T10, K 1 r.
C.off with latch tool.

BUTTONHOLE BAND
K as for buttonband, working 4 buttonholes evenly along 4th r.

WAISTCORD
C.on by hand 3 sts.
RC 000, MT, K 250 (260, 270, 300, 300) rs.
C.off.

TO MAKE UP
Insert sleeves, sew side & sleeve seams.
Thread ribbons through 3 rs of eyelets at hem & on bodice.
Attach lace to hem.
Thread cord through waist.
Sew buttons on back opening.
Press with warm iron.

Hot Air Balloon sweater.

(See photograph on page 24)

Sizes 81/91cm (32/36in)

Materials 1 cone BK Acrylic col A, Saxe blue
Small amounts BK, cols 001 Black, 002 White, 003 Brown, 004 Royal, 005 Red, 006 Cream, 007 Rust, 008 Beige, 009 Orange, 010 Grey, 018 Mid Green, 019 Primrose, 022 Pink, 024 Emerald, 030 Purple
Small amounts of Gold & Silver thread. Intarsia chart (page 26)

Tension 26 sts × 44 rs = 10cm (4in) over SS
T at approx 6
26 sts × 44 rs = 10cm (4in) over Intarsia
T at approx 5

BACK
Col A, c.on in 1 × 1 rib 141 sts.
RC 000, T2/2, K 26 rs.
Trans sts to M/bed.
RC 000, MT, K 130 rs.
Mark both edges
Cont to K until RC 240 rs.
C.off 40 sts beg next 2 rs.
Rel work on WY.

FRONT
Col A, c.on in 1 × 1 rib 141 sts.
RC 000, T2/2, K 26 rs.
Trans sts to M/bed.
Dec 1 st, RC 000, Intarsia T.
Work from chart to RC 130.
Mark both edges.
Cont to work from chart until RC 210.

Shape neck
With spare piece of col A, c.off cent 20 sts.
K all sts left of cent 0 onto WY & rel from mach.
Work last 10 rs of patt.
At same time
K 1 r.
C.off 4 sts at neck beg next r.
K 1 r.

C.off 2 sts beg next & foll 3rd rs until 40 sts rem.
Cont to K until RC 240 rs.
C.off rem 40 sts.
Complete left side, rev all shaping.

SLEEVES
Col A, c.on in 1 × 1 rib 67 sts.
RC 000, T2/2, K 26 rs.
Trans sts to M/bed.
RC 000, MT, K 4 rs.
Inc 1 st both ends next & foll 5th rs until 139 sts.
Cont to K until RC 186.
C.off loosely.
Join left shoulder.

NECKBAND
Col A, c.on in 1 × 1 rib 137 sts.
RC 000, T4/4, K 4 rs. T3/3, K 4 rs. T2/2, K 8 rs. T3/3, K 4 rs. T4/4, K 4 rs.
Trans sts to M/bed.
With wong side facing pick up sts, 61 from back, 8 neck shaping, 60 across front, 8 neck shaping.
MT, K 1 r. T10, K 1 r.
C.off with latch tool.

Hot Air Balloon sweater—see pattern on page 23

Owl sweater—see pattern on page 27

TO MAKE UP

Join right shoulder, insert sleeves between markers, sew side & sleeve seams.

Fold neckband to inside & slip st into pos.

Press with cool iron.

FINISH:

Balloon—lay silver thread in diagonal lines across bottom & secure at back.

With gold thread couch threads down at cross over on silver with small cross st.

Cut 2 lengths gold thread approx 81cm (32in) long.

Fold into 4 & secure from outer edges of balloon to basket.

Trees—using brown, stem st branches. Using emerald, lazy daisy st leaves onto branches.

Houses—using black & brown cross st, form doors & windows. Using green, red, yellow & pink, embroider flowers around doors & up the side of houses.

Grass—using different shades of green, Swiss darn length of col into grass.

Bird—using black, fly st birds onto clouds & sky.

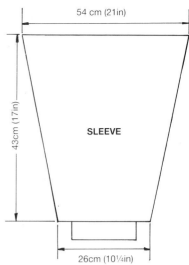

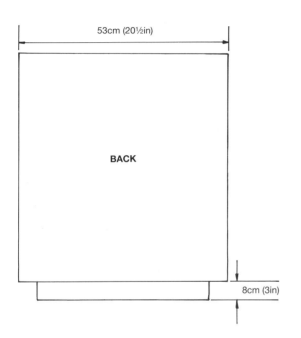

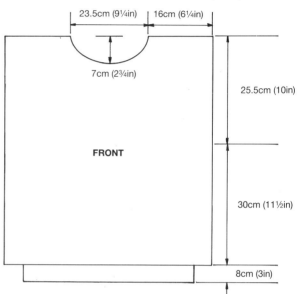

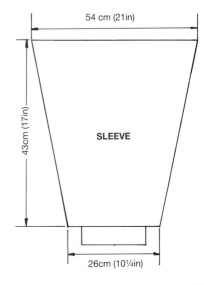

Owl sweater.

(See photograph on page 25)

Sizes 81/91cm (32/36in)

Materials 1 cone BK Acrylic col A Small amounts BK, cols 001 Black, 002 White, 003 Brown, 006 Cream, 007 Rust, 009 Orange

Small amounts of Gold & Silver thread

6mm (¼in) mother of pearl star sequins. Intarsia chart.

14mm (½in) mother of pearl star sequins

18mm (¾in) leaf gold sequins

5mm (¼in) black cup sequins

18mm (¾in) leaf silver silver sequins. Intarsia chart (page 29)

Tension 26 sts × 44 rs = 10cm (4in) over SS

T at approx 6

26 sts × 44 rs = 10cm (4in) over Intarsia

T at approx 5

BACK

Col A, c.on in 1 × 1 rib 141 sts.
RC 000, T2/2, K 26 rs.
Trans sts to M/bed.
RC 000, MT, K 130 rs.
Mark both edges.
Cont to K until RC 240 rs.
C.off 40 sts beg next 2 rs.
Rel work on WY.

FRONT

Col A, c.on in 1 × 1 rib 141 sts.
RC 000, T2/2, K 26 rs.
Trans sts to M/bed.
Dec 1 st.
RC 000, Intarsia T, work from chart to RC 130.
Mark both edges.
Cont to work from chart until RC 210.

Shape neck

With spare piece of col A, c.off cent 20 sts.
K all sts left of cent 0 onto WY & rel from mach.
Work last 10 rs of patt.

At same time

K 1 r. C.off 4 sts at neck beg next r. K 1 r.
C.off 2 sts beg next & foll 3rd rs until 40 sts rem.
Cont to K until RC 240 rs.
C.off rem 40 sts.
Complete left side, rev all shaping & working tree trunk.

SLEEVES

Col A, c.on in 1 × 1 rib 67 sts.
RC 000, T2/2, K 26 rs.
Trans sts to M/bed.
RC 000, MT, K 4 rs.
Inc 1 st both ends next & foll 5th rows until 139 sts.
Cont to K until RC 186.
C.off loosely.
Join left shoulder

NECKBAND

Col A, c.on in 1 × 1 rib 137 sts.
RC 000, T4/4, K 4 rs. T3/3, K 4 rs.
T2/2, K 8 rs. T3/3, K 4 rs. T4/4, K 4 rs.
Trans sts to M/bed.

With wrong side facing pick up sts, 61 from back, 8 neck shaping, 60 across front, 8 neck shaping.
MT, K 1 r. T10, K 1 r.
C.off with latch tool.

TO MAKE UP

Join right shoulder, insert sleeves between markers, sew side & sleeve seams.
Fold neckband to inside & slip st into pos.
Press with cool iron.

FINISH:
Sew mother of pearl star sequins at random in sky.
Sew leaf gold sequins onto breast of owl.
Sew leaf silver sequins on head as beak.
Sew black cup sequins on eyes, secure with small bead.
Outline wing with gold thread using stem st.
Decorate wing with gold thread.

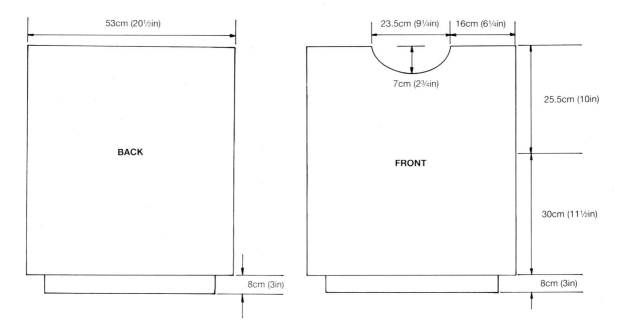

Striped Dolman sweater.

(See photograph on page 32)

Sizes 86/91 (97/102)cm (34/36 (38/40)in)

Materials 1 cone Bramwell Hobby col A
1 cone Bramwell Hobby col B
Small amount BK Charisma col C

Tension 26 sts × 56 rs = 10cm (4in)
T at approx 3

Note Purl side is right side of garment

BACK

To the right of cent 0 c.on in WY 51 (56) sts.
K few rs. Carr at left.
K 1 r in nylon cord.
Col A, RC 000, MT, inc 1 st at left ev 6th rs.
26 times in all. 77 (82) sts.
K 4 rs. Inc 1 st at left next r.
C.on 2 sts at left next & foll r.
C.on 3 sts at left next 3 rs.
C.on 40 sts beg next r.
RC 168. 130 (135) sts.
K 42 (52) rs.
Col B, K 20 rs. Col A, K 30 rs*.
Mark right edge for back neck.
Col B, K 20 rs. Col A, K 30 rs.
Col B, K 50 rs. Col A, K 30 rs.
Col B, K 20 rs.
Mark right edge for back neck **.
Col A, K 30 rs. Col B, K 20 rs.
Col A, K 43 (53) rs. RC 503 (523).
C.off 40 sts beg next r. K 1 r.
Cast off 3 sts at left next 3 rs.
Cast off 2 sts at left next 2 rs.
Dec 1 st at left next r. K 5 rs.
RC 516 (536).
Dec. 1 st at left next & foll 6th rs until 51 (55) sts rem.
K 3 rs. RC 670 (680).
Rel work on WY.

FRONT

K as for back to *.

Shape neck
RC 260 (270).

Keeping stripe patt correct dec 1 st at right next & foll alt rs 10 times in all.
Work 110 rs.
Inc. 1 st at right next & foll alt rs 10 times in all.
RC 410 (420).
Work as for back from **.

CUFFS
(K two)
Col C, c.on in 1 × 1 rib 61 (65) sts.
RC 000, T1/1, K 40 rs.
Trans sts to M/bed.
With knit side facing pick up sts evenly around sleeve edge.
T5, K 1 r. T10, K 1 r.
C.off with latch tool.

WELTS
(K two)
Col C, c.on in 1 × 1 rib 129 (133) sts.
RC 000, T1/1, K 40 rs.
Trans sts to M/bed.
With knit side facing pick up sts evenly from front or back waist.

T5, K 1 r. T10, K 1 r.
C.off with latch tool.

COLLAR
Bring forward 150 ns
Using 1 strand of col A & 1 strand of col B with purl side facing pick up sts evenly from front and back neck.
RC 000, MT + 2, K 18 rs.

Work trianges
Push 125 sts at left into HP.
*Work on 25 sts at right.
Dec 1 st both ends next & foll alt rs until all sts have been dec*.
Bring next 25 sts at right back into WP and work from * to *.
Repeat 4 more times.

TO MAKE UP
Block & steam press all pieces.
Join upper and lower sleeve seams.
Fold collar to front.
Work 2 rs double crochet around points using col C.

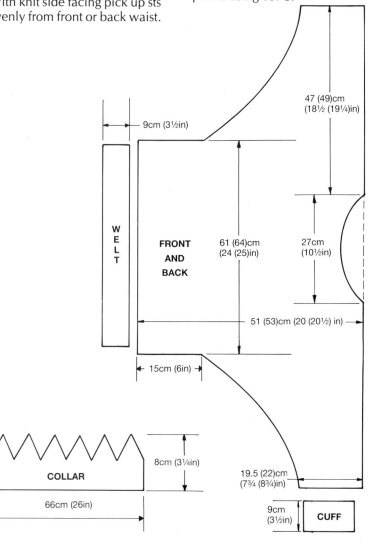

Batwing sweater & leg warmers.

(See photograph on page 33)

Sizes 81/86 (91/107)cm (32/36 (38/42)in)

Materials 2 cones BK Charisma

Tension 28 sts × 40 rs = 10cm (4in)
T at approx 6

BACK

To the right of cent 0, c.on in WY 55 (60) sts.
K few rs. Carr at left.
K 1 r in nylon cord.
MY, RC 000, MT, K 30 rs.
Inc 1 st at left next & foll alt rs 50 times in all until RC 130.
K 1 r. Carr at left.
C.on 25 sts beg next r.
RC 132. 130 (135) sts.
K 96 (106) rs. RC 228 (238)*.
Mark right edge for back neck.
K 80 rs. Mark right edge.
** K 97 (107) rs.
C.off 25 sts at left.
Dec 1 st at left next & foll alt rs until 55 (60) sts rem.
K 30 rs. RC 536 (556).
Rel work on WY.

FRONT

K as for back to *. RC 228 (238).

Shape neck
Dec 1 st at right next 8 rs.
K 64 rs.
Inc 1 st at right next 8 rs.
K as for back from ** to end.

CUFFS
(K two)
C.on in 1 × 1 rib 61 (65) sts.
RC 000, T1/1, K 30 rs.
Trans sts to M/bed.
With wrong side facing, pick up sts evenly around sleeve edge.
T7, K 1 r. T10, K 1 r.
C.off with latch tool.

WELTS
(K two)
C.on in 1 × 1 rib 127 sts.
RC 000, T1/1, K 40 rs.
Trans sts to M/bed.
With wrong side facing, pick up sts evenly along front or back waist.
MT, K 1 r. T10, K 1 r.
C.off with latch tool.

NECKBAND
C.on in 1 × 1 rib 151 sts.
RC 000, T5/5, K 10 rs.
T4/4, K 30 rs. T3/3, K 50 rs.
T2/2, K 50 rs.
Trans sts to M/bed.
With wrong side facing, pick up sts evenly around neck.
T7, K 1 r. T10, K 1 r.
C.off with latch tool.

Leg Warmers
C.on in 1 × 1 rib 71 sts.
RC 000, T1/1, K 40 rs.
Trans sts to M/bed.
RC 000, MT. Inc 1 st both ends next & ev foll 8th rs until 111 sts.
Cont to K to RC 160.
Trans sts to 1 × 1 rib.
T1/1, K 40 rs.
C.off.

TO MAKE UP
Join inside seam.
Fold top rib to outside.
Press.

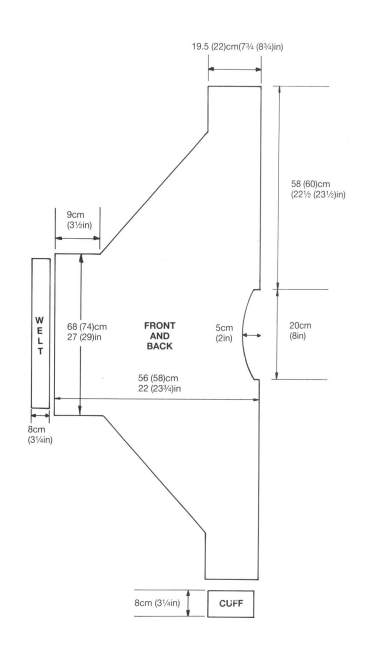

19.5 (22)cm(7¾ (8¾)in)

58 (60)cm (22½ (23½)in)

9cm (3½in)

68 (74)cm 27 (29)in

FRONT AND BACK

WELT

5cm (2in)

20cm (8in)

56 (58)cm 22 (23¾)in

8cm (3¼in)

8cm (3¼in)

CUFF

Striped Dolman sweater—see pattern on page 30

Batwing sweater and leg warmers—see pattern on page 31

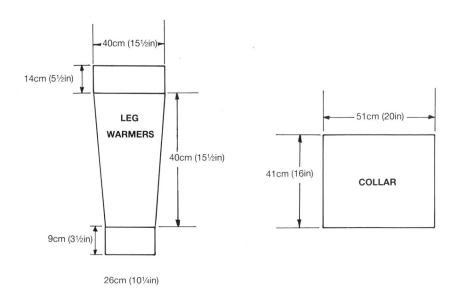

LEG
WARMERS

40cm (15½in)

14cm (5½in)

40cm (15½in)

9cm (3½in)

26cm (10¼in)

COLLAR

51cm (20in)

41cm (16in)

Fairisle sweater.

(See photograph on page 36)

Sizes 81 (86, 91, 97, 102)cm (32 (34, 36, 38, 40)in)

Materials 1 cone BK 4-ply col A
1 cone BK 4-ply col B
cards 4 and 5
3 buttons

Tension 28 sts × 40 rs = 10cm (4in) over SS
T at approx 6

BACK
Col A, c.on in 1 × 1 rib 123 (129, 135, 141, 147) sts.
RC 000, T1/1, K 40 rs.
Trans sts to M/bed. Inc 1 st.
RC 000, MT, K 116 rs.

Shape armhole
C.off 8 (9, 10, 11, 12) sts beg next 2 rs.
C.off 2 sts beg next 2 rs.
C.off 1 st beg next 6 rs.
Cont to K until RC 172.

Divide for back opening
C.off cent 2 sts.
Place all sts left cent into HP or K back onto nylon cord.
Cont to K on right side only.
K until RC 187.

Shape neck
C.off 13 sts at neck edge.
K 1 r. Dec 1 st at neck next 5 rs.

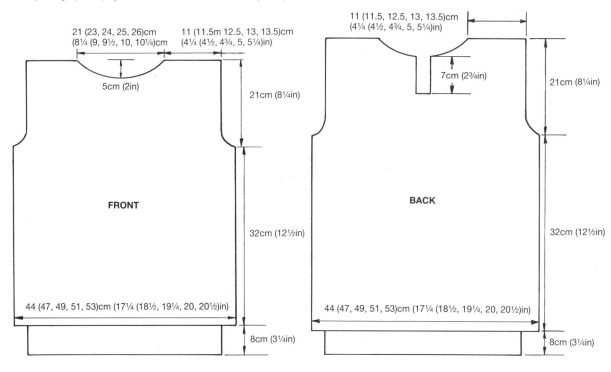

21 (23, 24, 25, 26)cm (8¼ (9, 9½, 10, 10¼)cm

11 (11.5m 12.5, 13, 13.5)cm (4¼ (4½, 4¾, 5, 5¼)in)

5cm (2in)

21cm (8¼in)

FRONT

32cm (12½in)

44 (47, 49, 51, 53)cm (17¼ (18½, 19¼, 20, 20½)in)

8cm (3¼in)

11 (11.5, 12.5, 13, 13.5)cm (4¼ (4½, 4¾, 5, 5¼)in)

7cm (2¾in)

21cm (8¼in)

BACK

32cm (12½in)

44 (47, 49, 51, 53)cm (17¼ (18½, 19¼, 20, 20½)in)

8cm (3¼in)

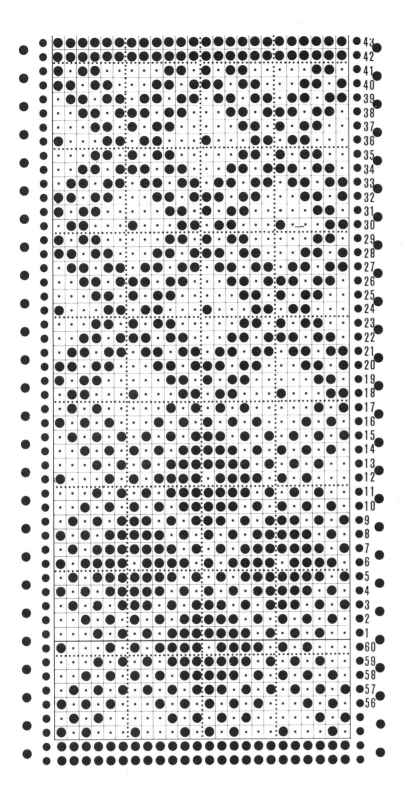

Above: card 4

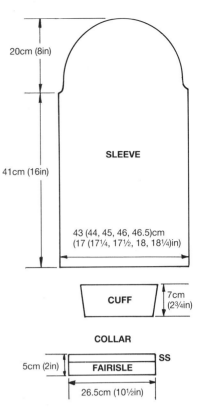

20cm (8in)

41cm (16in)

SLEEVE

43 (44, 45, 46, 46.5)cm
(17 (17¼, 17½, 18, 18¼)in)

CUFF

7cm
(2¾in)

COLLAR

5cm (2in)

SS

FAIRISLE

26.5cm (10½in)

K 1 r.
RC 194.

Shape shoulders
C.off 10 sts beg next & foll alt rs.
K 1 r.
C.off rem 10 (12, 14, 16, 18) sts.
Work left side to match rev
shaping.

FRONT
Insert card 4 & lock to K row 1.
Col A, c.on in 1 × 1 rib 123 (129,
135, 141, 147) sts.
RC 000, T1/1, K 40 rs.
Trans sts to M/bed. Inc 1 st.
RC 000, MT.
Rel card & work in fairisle until
RC 116.

Shape armhole
C.off 8 (9, 10, 11, 12) sts beg next
2 rs.
C.off 2 sts beg next 2 rs.
C.off 1 st beg next 6 rs.
Cont to K until RC 178.

Shape neck
C.off cent 16 sts.
Place all sts left of cent 0 into HP
or K back onto nylon cord.
MARK CARD ROW NO.
Dec 1 st at neck next 6 rs.
Dec 1 st at neck next & foll alt rs 5
times in all until 30 (32, 34, 36,
38) sts rem.

Fairisle sweater—see pattern on page 34

Shape shoulder

C.off 10 sts beg next & foll alt rs.
K 1 r.
C.off rem 10 (12, 14, 16, 18) sts.
Reset card & work left side to match.

SLEEVES

C. on in WY 120 (122, 124, 126, 128) sts.
K few rs. Carr at left.
K 1 r in nylon cord.
RC 000, MT, SS, K 140 (144, 148, 152, 156) rs.

Shape top

C.off 8 (9, 10, 11, 12) sts beg next 2 rs.
Dec 1 st both ends next & foll alt rs until 70 sts rem.
C.off 2 sts beg next 20 rs.
C.off rem sts.

CUFFS

(K two)
Bring forward 60 (61, 62, 63, 64) ns.
With wrong side facing pick up sts evenly around sleeve edge placing 2 sts on each n.
Col A, MT-2, K 10 rs. MT-3, K 15 rs.
MT-4, K 14 rs. T10, K 1 r.
MT-4, K 14 rs. MT-3, K 15 rs.
MT-2, K 10 rs. T10, K 1 r.
C.off with latch tool.

COLLAR

(K two)
Join shoulder seams.
Bring forward 50 ns.
With right side facing pick up sts evenly from cent front to cent back.
Insert card 5 & lock to K row 1.
Col A, RC 000, MT-2, K 10 rs.
Rel card & work in fairisle.
MT, K 13 rs. SS, K 1 r.
C.off.

TO MAKE UP

Insert sleeves.
Sew side & sleeve seams, fold cuffs to inside & slip st into pos.
Col A, work 2 rs double crochet around collar & back neck opening working 2 buttonholes on right.
Sew on buttons.
Press with warm iron.

Right: card 5

Ski sweater & hat.

(See photograph on page 40)

Sizes 81/86 (91/97, 102/107)cm
(32/34 (36/38, 40/42)in)

Materials 2 (2, 2) cones BK
Superwash Wool col A
Small amount col B
Card 6

Tension 32 sts × 44 rs = 10cm
(4in)
T at approx 6

BACK
Col A, c.on in 1 × 1 rib 143 (147,
151) sts.
RC 000, T1/1, K 40 rs.
Trans sts to M/bed.
RC 000, MT, K 140 rs.

Shape armholes
C.off 10 sts beg next 2 rs.
Cont to K until RC 236.

Shape shoulders
C.off 30 (32, 34) sts beg next 2 rs.
Rel work on WY.

FRONT
Insert card & lock to K row 1.
Col A, c.on in 1 × 1 rib 143 (147,
151) sts.
RC 000, T1/1, K 40 rs.
Trans sts to M/bed.
RC 000, MT, K 6 rs.
Rel card & work 1 complete
rotation.
Cont to work in SS until RC 140.

Shape armholes
C.off 10 sts beg next 2 rs.
Cont to K until RC 196.

Shape neck
Push 69 (71, 73) sts at left into HP
or K back onto nylon cord.
Work on right side only, always
taking yarn round last n in HP.
K 2 rs.
AT NECK EDGE

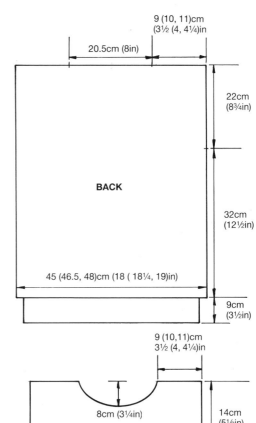

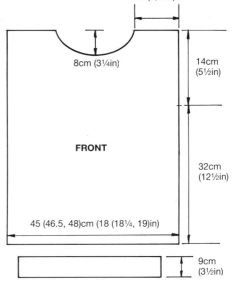

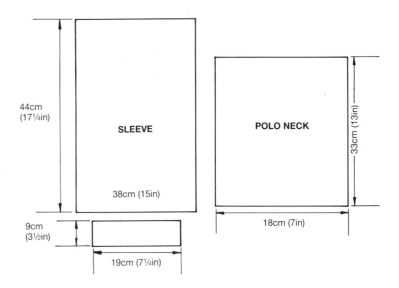

Push 6 sts into HP next r. K 1 r.
Push 4 sts into HP next r. K 1 r.
Push 2 sts into HP next & foll alt rs
5 times in all.
Push 1 st into HP next & foll alt rs
4 times in all until 30 (32, 34) sts
rem.
Cont to K until RC 236.
C.off rem sts.
Leave cent 15 sts in HP and work
left side to match.
Rel cent sts on WY.

SLEEVES
WY, c.on 140 sts.
K few rs. Carr at left.
K 1 r in nylon cord.
Col A, RC 000, MT, K 190 rs.
C.off loosely.

CUFFS
(K two)
Col A, c.on in 1 × 1 rib 61 sts.
RC 000, T1/1, K 50 rs.
Trans sts to M/bed.
With wrong side facing pick up
sts evenly from sleeve.
T7, K 1 r. T10, K 1 r.
C.off with latch tool.

NECKBAND
Col A, C.on in 1 × 1 rib 151 sts.
RC 000, T4/4, K 20 rs.
T3/3, K 30 rs. T2/2, K 30 rs.
T1/1, K 50 rs.
Trans sts to M/bed.
With wrong side facing pick up
sts from back and front neck.
T7, K 1 r. T10, K 1 r.
C.off with latch tool.

TO MAKE UP
Block & steam press.
Join shoulder seams.
Insert sleeves.
Sew side & sleeve seams.
Join half of polo neck leaving rest
open. Col B, work 2 rs double
crochet around opening and c.on-
edge of collar.
Press.

Hat
Col A, c.on in 1 × 1 rib 139 sts.
RC 000, T4/4, K 30 rs.
T3/3, K 20 rs.
T2/2, K 70 rs.
Trans sts to M/bed.
Insert card & lock to K row 18.
RC 000, K 6 rs. Rel card & work 2
complete skier motifs.
Cont in SS, K 6 rs.
Carr at right.
Push 105 ns at left into HP or K

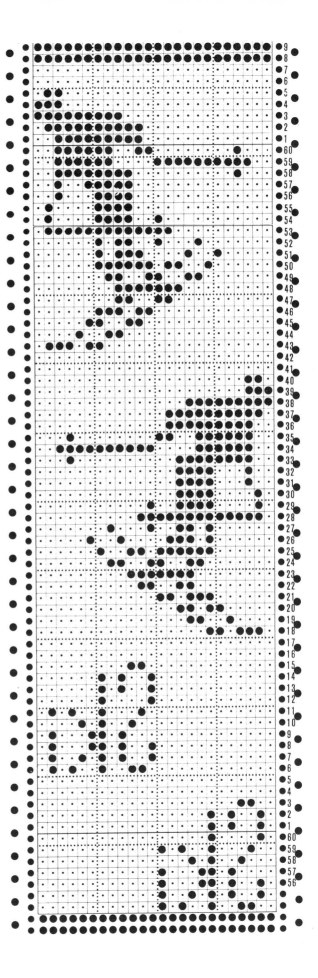

back onto nylon cord.
Work on right only.
Col A, dec 1 st both ends next &
ev foll alt rs until all sts have been
dec.
*Bring next 35 sts back into WP.
Col B, dec 1 st both ends next &
foll alt rs until all sts have been
dec*.
Work from * to * once in col A,
then again in col B.

TO MAKE UP
Block and steam press.
Sew top seams.
Join side seam.
Make pom pom in cols A & B and
attach to top.

Tuck stitch top.

(See photograph on page 44)

Sizes 81 (86, 91, 97, 102)cm (32 (34, 36, 38, 40)in)

Materials 1 cone Bramwell Artistic col A
Small amount Bramwell Artistic col B
Card 7

Tension 26 sts × 40 rs = 10cm (4in) over patt
T at approx 7 (pressed)

FRONT
Insert card & lock to K row 1.
Col B, c.on in 1 × 1 rib 111 (117, 123, 129, 135) sts.
RC 000, T1/1, K 10 rs.
Trans sts to M/bed. Inc 1 st.
RC 000, MT.
Rel card & work in tuck patt, col A, K 86 (90, 90, 90, 96) rs.

Shape armholes
C.off 6 sts beg next 2 rs.
Dec 1 st both ends next & foll alt rs 6 times in all 88 (94, 100, 106, 112) sts rem.
Cont to K until RC 126 (136, 140, 146, 156).

Shape neck
C.off cent 20 sts.
Place all sts at left into HP or K back onto nylon cord.
Work on right side only.
MARK CARD ROW NO.
Dec. 1 st at cent next 6 rs.
Dec 1 st at cent next & foll alt rs 7 times in all until 21 (24, 27, 30, 33) sts rem.
Cont to K until RC 156 (166, 170, 176, 186).

Shape shoulder
C.off 5 (6, 7, 7, 8) sts beg next & foll alt rs 3 times in all. K 1 r.
C.off rem 6 (6, 6, 7, 8) sts.

Reset card and work on left side rev shaping.

LEFT BACK & TIE
Insert card & lock to K row 1.
Col B, c.on in 1 × 1 rib 135 (139, 141, 145, 147) sts.
RC 000, T1/1, K 10 rs.
C.off 79 sts at left.
Trans sts to M/bed.
RC 000, MT.
Rel card & work in tuck patt, col A, K 86 (90, 90, 90, 96) rs.

Shape armhole
C.off 6 sts beg next r. K 1 r.
Dec 1 st beg next & foll alt rs 6 (6, 6, 6, 3) times in all until 44 (48, 50, 54, 59) sts rem.

Cont to K until RC 145 (155, 159, 165, 175).

Shape neck
C.off 18 sts beg next r. K 1 r.
Dec 1 st at neck next 5 (6, 5, 6, 8) rs until 21 (24, 27, 30, 33) sts rem.
Cont to K until RC 156 (166, 170, 176, 186).

Shape shoulder
C.off 5 (6, 7, 7, 8) sts beg next & foll alt rs 3 times in all.
C.off rem 6 (6, 6, 7, 8) sts.
Work right front as for left rev all shaping.

NECKBAND
Col B, c.on in 1 × 1 rib 117 sts.

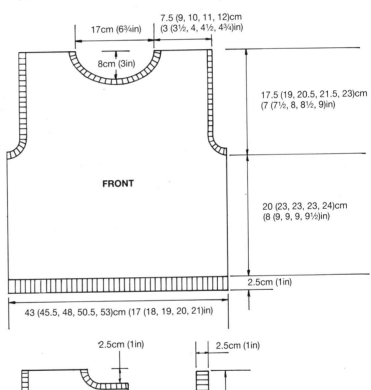

7.5 (9, 10, 11, 12)cm (3 (3½, 4, 4½, 4¾)in)

17cm (6¾in)

8cm (3in)

17.5 (19, 20.5, 21.5, 23)cm (7 (7½, 8, 8½, 9)in)

FRONT

20 (23, 23, 23, 24)cm (8 (9, 9, 9, 9½)in)

2.5cm (1in)

43 (45.5, 48, 50.5, 53)cm (17 (18, 19, 20, 21)in)

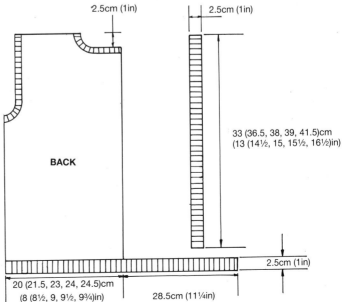

2.5cm (1in)

2.5cm (1in)

33 (36.5, 38, 39, 41.5)cm (13 (14½, 15, 15½, 16½)in)

BACK

2.5cm (1in)

20 (21.5, 23, 24, 24.5)cm (8 (8½, 9, 9½, 9¾)in)

28.5cm (11¼in)

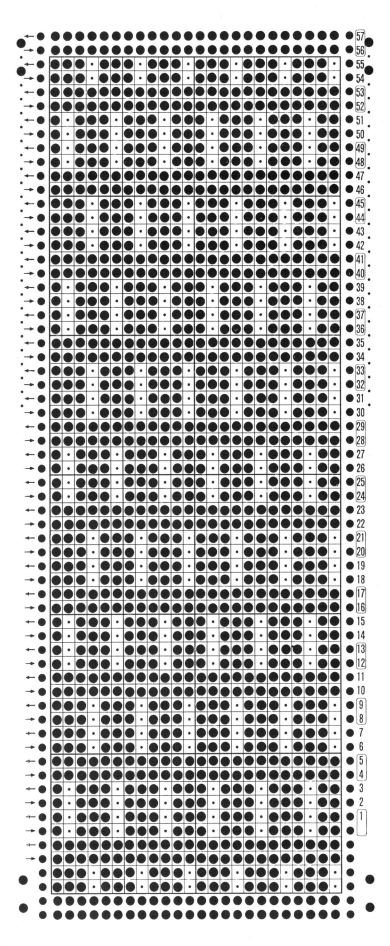

RC 000, T2/2, K 8 rs.
T4/4, K 2 rs.
Trans sts to M/bed.
With knit side facing, pick up sts
around neck.
MT, K 1 r. T10, K 1 r.
C.off with latch tool.

ARMBANDS

(K two)
Join shoulder seams.
Col B, c.on in 1 × 1 rib 105 (117,
121, 131, 137) sts.
RC 000, T2/2, K 8 rs.
T4/4, K 2 rs.
Trans sts to M/bed.
With knit side facing, pick up sts
evenly around armhole.
MT, K 1 r. T10, K 1 r.
C.off with latch tool.

BACKBANDS

Left

Col B, c.on in 1 × 1 rib 91 (95,
101, 105, 111) sts.
RC 000, T2/2, K 8 rs.
T4/4, K 2 rs.
Trans sts to M/bed.
With knit side facing, pick up sts
evenly along back.
MT, K 1 r. T10, K 1 r.
C.off with latch tool.

Right

K. as for left band working small
buttonhole on 6th st at top.

TO MAKE UP

Press lightly with steam iron.
Sew side seams.
Sew button to top.
Tie back waist.

Tuck stitch beaded top.

(See photograph on page 44)

Sizes 81 (86, 91, 97, 102)cm (32 (34, 36, 38, 40)in)

Materials 1 cone Bramwell Artistic col A
Small amount Bramwell Artistic col B
Card 8
1 pack beads

Tension 26 sts × 40 rs = 10cm (4in) over patt
T at approx 7 (pressed)

Note RC 40—work first bead onto cent tuck patt.
Work 3 beads onto 8th row tuck patt, 8 sts apart each side cent.
Work 5 beads onto 8th row tuck patt, 8 sts apart.
Cont until 11 beads have been worked across row.
Cont working 11 beads onto 8th row until end.

FRONT

Insert card & lock to K row 1.
Col B, c.on in 1 × 1 rib 111 (117, 123, 129, 135) sts.
RC 000, T1/1, K 10 rs.
Trans sts to M/bed. Inc 1 st.
RC 000, MT.
Rel card & work in tuck patt, col A.
From RC 40 work beads onto front until RC reads 86 (90, 90, 90, 96).

Shape armholes

C.off 6 sts beg next 2 rs.
Dec 1 st both ends next & foll alt rs, 6 times in all.
88 (94, 100, 106, 112) sts rem.
Cont to K until RC 126 (136, 140, 146, 156).

Shape neck

C.off cent 20 sts.

Place all sts at left into HP or K back onto nylon cord.
Work on right side only.
MARK CARD ROW NO.
Dec 1 st at cent next 6 rs.
Dec 1 st at cent next and foll alt rs, 7 times in all.
21 (24, 27, 30, 33) sts rem.
Cont to K until RC 156 (166, 170, 176, 186).

Shape shoulder

C.off 5 (6, 7, 7, 8) sts beg next & foll alt rs, 3 times in all.
K 1 r.
C.off rem 6 (6, 6, 7, 8) sts.
Reset card and work on left side, rev shaping.

LEFT BACK & TIE

Insert card & lock to K row 1.
Col B, c.on in 1 × 1 rib 135 (139, 141, 145, 147) sts.
RC 000, T1/1, K 10 rs.
C.off 79 sts at left.
Trans sts to M/bed.
RC 000, MT.
Rel card & work in tuck patt, col A.
K 86 (90, 90, 90, 96) rs.

Shape armhole

C.off 6 sts beg next r. K 1 r.
Dec 1 st beg next & foll alt rs, 6 times in all.
50 (54, 56, 60, 62) sts rem.
Cont to K until RC 145 (155, 159, 165, 175).

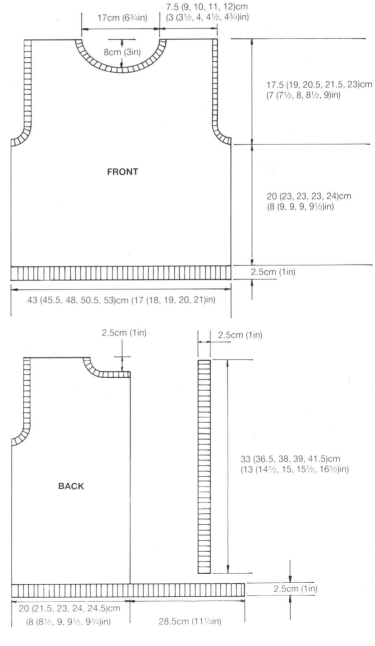

7.5 (9, 10, 11, 12)cm (3 (3½, 4, 4½, 4¾)in)

17cm (6¾in)

8cm (3in)

17.5 (19, 20.5, 21.5, 23)cm (7 (7½, 8, 8½, 9)in)

FRONT

20 (23, 23, 23, 24)cm (8 (9, 9, 9, 9½)in)

2.5cm (1in)

43 (45.5, 48, 50.5, 53)cm (17 (18, 19, 20, 21)in)

2.5cm (1in)

2.5cm (1in)

33 (36.5, 38, 39, 41.5)cm (13 (14½, 15, 15½, 16½)in)

BACK

2.5cm (1in)

20 (21.5, 23, 24, 24.5)cm (8 (8½, 9, 9½, 9¾)in)

28.5cm (11¼in)

Tuck stitch top and tuck stitch beaded top—see patterns on pages 41 and 43

Shape neck

C.off 18 sts beg next r. K 1 r.
Dec 1 st at neck edge next 5 (6, 5, 6, 8) rs.
21 (24, 27, 30, 33) sts rem.
Cont to K until RC 156 (166, 170, 176, 186).

Shape shoulder

C.off 5 (6, 7, 7, 8) sts beg next & foll alt rs, 3 times in all.
C.off rem 6 (6, 6, 7, 8) sts.
Work right front as for left, rev all shaping.

NECKBAND

Col B, c.on in 1 × 1 rib 127 sts.
RC 000, T2/2, K 8 rs.
T4/4, K 2 rs.
Trans sts to M/bed.
With knit side facing, pick up sts around neck.
MT, K 1 r. T10, K 1 r.
C.off with latch tool.

ARMBANDS

Join shoulder seams.
Col B, c.on in 1 × 1 rib 115 (117, 131, 141, 147) sts.
RC 000, T2/2, K 8 rs.
T4/4, K 2 rs.
Trans sts to M/bed.
With knit side facing, pick up sts evenly around armhole.
MT, K 1 r. T10, K 1 r.
C.off with latch tool.

BACKBANDS

Left

Col B, c.on in 1 × 1 rib 91 (95, 101, 105, 111) sts.
RC 000, T2/2, K 8 rs.
T4/4, K 2 rs.
Trans sts to M/bed.
With knit side facing, pick up sts evenly along back.
MT, K 1 r. T10, K 1 r.
C.off with latch tool.

Right

K as for left band working small buttonhole on 5th row 6th st from top.

TO MAKE UP

Press lightly with steam iron.
Sew side seams.
Sew button to top.
Tie back waist.

Summer top.

(See photograph on page 48)

Sizes 81 (86, 91, 97, 102)cm (32 (34, 36, 38, 40)in)

Materials 2 cones BK Shimmer used two ends throughout
Card 9
3 buttons

Tension 26 sts × 40 rs = 10cm (4in) over patt lightly pressed
T at approx 7

BACK
Insert card & lock to K row 1.
C.on in 1 × 1 rib 111 (117, 123, 129, 135) sts.
RC 000, T1/1, K 20 rs.
Trans sts to M/bed. Inc 1 st.
RC 000, MT.
Rel card & work in tuck patt. K 116 rs*.

Shape top
RC 000, c.off 3 (3, 4, 5, 5) sts beg next 2 rs.
Dec 1 st both ends next & foll 4th rs 16 times in all. K 1 r.
74 (80, 84, 88, 94) sts rem.
Dec 1 st both ends next & foll alt rs 14 (16, 16, 16, 18) times until 46 (48, 52, 54, 58) sts rem.
RC 92 (96, 96, 96, 100).
C.off rem sts.

FRONT
K as for back to *. RC 116.

Shape top
RC 000, c.off 3 (3, 4, 5, 5) sts beg next 2 rs.
Dec 1 st both ends next & foll 4th rs, 3 times in all.
K 1 r. RC 12.
MARK CARD ROW NO.

Divide work for neck opening
C.off cent 8 sts.
K all sts at left back onto nylon

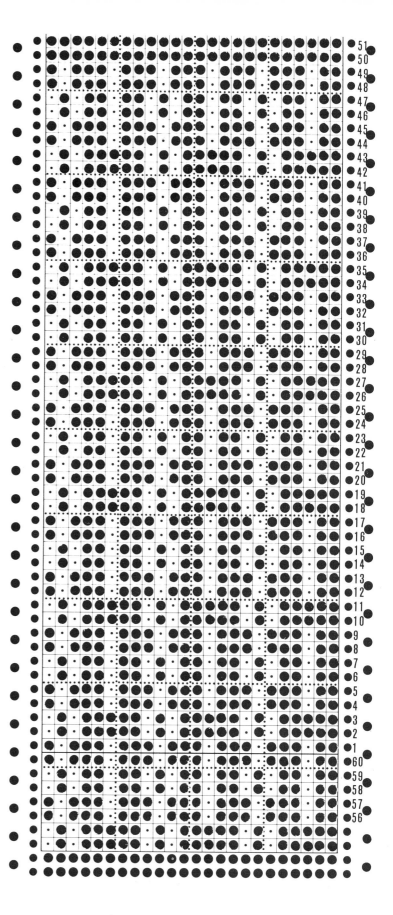

cord or rel on WY.
Work on right side only.
Cont to dec 1 st at armhole ev 4th
rs until 33 (36, 38, 40, 43) sts
rem.
Dec 1 st at armhole edge next &
foll alt rs until RC 72 (76, 76, 76,
80).

Shape neck

Cont to dec ev alt rs at armhole
edge and **at same time**
C.off 10 sts at neck beg next r.
K 1 r.
C.off 3 (4, 6, 8, 9) sts beg next r.
K 1 r.
Dec 1 st at cent next & foll alt rs,
6 times in all.
Cont to dec 1 st at armhole edge
until all sts have been dec.
RC 92 (96, 96, 96, 100).
Reset card.
Work left side to match rev
shaping.

FRONT BANDS

(K two)
C.on in 1 × 1 rib 37 (39, 39, 39,
43) sts.
TC 000, T2/2, K 12 rs.
Trans sts to M/bed.
With wrong side facing pick up
sts from left side cent to neck.
MT, K 1 r. T10, K 1 r.
C.off with latch tool.
Work button band to match
working 3, 2 st button holes along
7th r.

COLLAR

Join right shoulder.
C.on in 1 × 1 rib 113 (121, 129,
135, 139) sts.
RC 000, T3/3, K 12 rs. T2/2, K 12
rs. T1/1, K 18 rs.
Trans sts to M/bed.
With wrong side facing pick up
sts from neck edge starting at front
neck shaping across back and
down front neck shaping.
MT, K 1 r. T10, K 1 r.
C.off with latch tool.

ARMBANDS

(K two)
C.on in 1 × 1 rib 135 (141, 149,
155, 161) sts.
RC 000, T2/2, K 12 rs.
Trans sts to M/bed.
With wrong side facing pick up
sts evenly around armholes.
MT, K 1 r. T10, K 1 r.
C.off with latch tool.

TO MAKE UP

Join shoulder and bands.
Sew bands to cent front.
Sew side seams.
Sew buttons to front.
Press lightly.

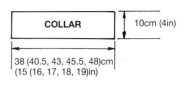

COLLAR

10cm (4in)

38 (40.5, 43, 45.5, 48)cm
(15 (16, 17, 18, 19)in)

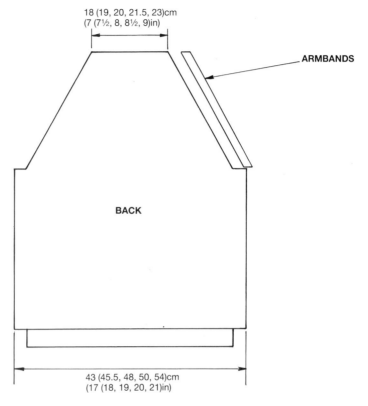

18 (19, 20, 21.5, 23)cm
(7 (7½, 8, 8½, 9)in)

ARMBANDS

BACK

43 (45.5, 48, 50, 54)cm
(17 (18, 19, 20, 21)in)

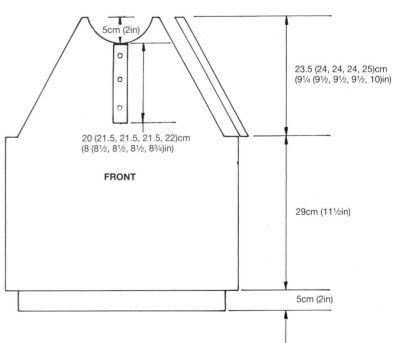

5cm (2in)

23.5 (24, 24, 24, 25)cm
(9¼ (9½, 9½, 9½, 10)in)

20 (21.5, 21.5, 21.5, 22)cm
(8 (8½, 8½, 8½, 8¾)in)

FRONT

29cm (11½in)

5cm (2in)

Summer top—see pattern on page 46

T-shirt—see pattern on page 50

T shirt.

(See photograph on page 49)

Sizes 81 (86, 91)cm (32 (34, 36)in)

Materials 1 cone Argyll Tica

Tension 28 sts × 48 rs = 10cm (4in)
T at approx 6

BACK

C.on in 1 × 1 rib 115 (121, 129) sts.
RC 000, T2/2, K 10 rs.
Trans sts to M/bed. Inc 1 st.
RC 000, MT, K 60 rs *.

Shape armholes

C.off 5 sts beg next 2 rs.
C.off 3 (3,4) sts beg next 2 rs.
Dec 1 st both ends next & foll alt rs until 40 (46, 52) sts rem.
RC 124.
Inc 1 st both ends next & foll alt rs, 12 times in all.
K 2 rs. RC 150.

Shape neck

Push 43 (48, 52) sts at left into HP or K back onto nylon cord.
Work on right side only.
Dec 1 st at cent next & foll alt rs, 15 times in all until 6 (7, 9) sts rem.
K 2 (6, 10) rs.
RC 182 (186, 190).
C.off.
Work left side to match rev shaping.
Rel cent sts on WY.

FRONT

K as for back to *. RC 60.

Shape armholes

C.off 5 sts beg next 2 rs.
C.off 3 (3,4) sts beg next 2 rs.
Dec 1 st both ends next & foll 4th rs until 60 (70, 76) sts rem.

Cont to K until RC 150.

Shape neck

Push 43 (48, 52) sts at left into HP or K back onto nylon cord.
Work on right side only.
Dec 1 st at cent next & foll alt rs, 15 times in all until 6 (7, 9) sts rem.
K2 (6, 10) rs.
RC 182 (186, 190).

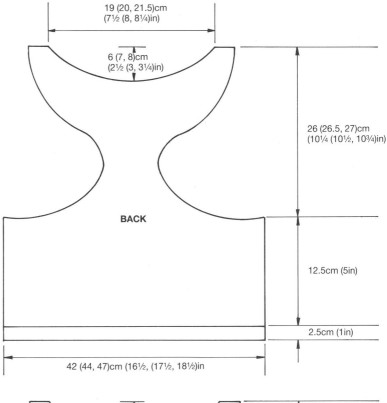

19 (20, 21.5)cm (7½ (8, 8¼)in)

6 (7, 8)cm (2½ (3, 3¼)in)

26 (26.5, 27)cm (10¼ (10½, 10¾)in)

BACK

12.5cm (5in)

2.5cm (1in)

42 (44, 47)cm (16½, (17½, 18½)in

C.off rem sts.
Work left side to match rev all shaping.
Rel cent sts on WY.

NECKBAND

Join right shoulder seam.
C.on in 1 × 1 rib 109 (125, 137) sts.
RC 000, T1/1, K 4 rs.
T2/2, K 6 rs.

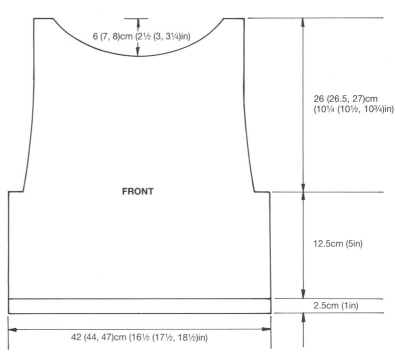

6 (7, 8)cm (2½ (3, 3¼)in)

26 (26.5, 27)cm (10¼ (10½, 10¾)in)

FRONT

12.5cm (5in)

2.5cm (1in)

42 (44, 47)cm (16½ (17½, 18½)in)

Trans sts to M/bed.
With wrong side facing pick up sts evenly around neck.
MT, K 1 r. T10, K 1 r.
C.off with latch tool.

ARMBANDS
(K two)
Join left shoulder seam.

C.on in 1 × 1 rib 169 (175, 181) sts.
RC 000, T1/1, K 4 rs.
T2/2, K 6 rs.
Trans sts to M/bed.
With wrong side facing pick up sts evenly around armholes 81 (85, 89) from front & 88 (90, 92) from back.

MT, K 1 r. T10, K 1 r.
C.off with latch tool.

TO MAKE UP
Join side seams.
Press.

HP or K back onto nylon cord.
*Always taking yarn round last ns in HP at oppos end to carr push 5 sts into HP next r. K 1 r.
Push 4 sts into HP next r. K 1 r.
Push 3 sts into HP next r. K 1 r.
Push 2 sts into HP next r. K 1 r.

Push 1 st into HP next & foll alt rs 6 times in all.
Cont to dec at armhole until 8 sts rem.
C.off.
Leave cent 16 sts in HP & rep shaping for other side.

(See photograph on page 52)

Sizes 81/86 (92/97)cm (32/34 (36/38)in)

Materials 1 cone each Argyll cotton cols A, B, C & D
4 buttons

Tension 32 sts × 44 rs = 10cm (4in) pressed
T at approx 5

Top

BACK & FRONT ALIKE
(K two)
Col A, c.on in 1 × 1 rib 131 (147) sts.
RC 000, T1/1, K 12 rs.
Trans sts to M/bed. Inc 1 st.
RC 000, MT, K 64 (68) rs.

Shape top
RC 000, c.off 2 (3) sts beg next 2 rs.
Dec 1 st at both ends next & foll 4th rs 17 (15) times in all.
RC 70 (62).
Dec 1 st at both edges next & foll alt rs 0 (7) times until RC 70 (76)*.

Shape neck
Work on right side only.
Cont to dec 1 st at armhole next & foll alt rs.
At same time
push cent 16 and all sts at left into

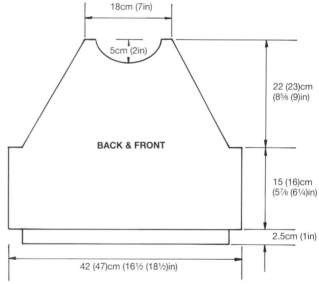

18cm (7in)

5cm (2in)

22 (23)cm (8⅝ (9)in)

BACK & FRONT

15 (16)cm (5⅞ (6¼)in)

2.5cm (1in)

42 (47)cm (16½ (18½)in)

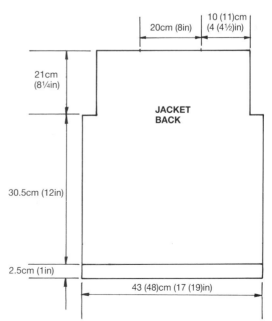

20cm (8in)

10 (11)cm (4 (4½)in)

21cm (8¼in)

JACKET BACK

30.5cm (12in)

2.5cm (1in)

43 (48)cm (17 (19)in)

Summer Twin Set—see pattern on page 51

K 1 r across all ns in HP.

Neckband
Trans sts to 1 × 1 rib.
T3/3, K 4 rs. T2/2, K 4 rs.
T1/1, K 4 rs.
C.off.

TO MAKE UP
Sew side seams.
Work 2 rs double crochet across
shoulders working 2 buttonhole
loops at front.
Press.

Jacket
Work in stripes as follows:
*Col B, K 2 rs. Col A, K 2 rs.
Col C, K 2 rs. Col A, K 18 rs.
Col D, K 2 rs. Col A, K 2 rs.
Col B, K 6 rs. Col D, K 2 rs.
Col C, K 4 rs. Col B, K 2 rs.
Col C, K 4 rs. Col D, K 2 rs.
Col A, K 18 rs*.

BACK
Col A, c.on in 1 × 1 rib 135 (151)
sts.
RC 000, T2/2, K 12 rs.
Trans sts to M/bed. Inc 1 st.
RC 000, MT.
Working in stripe patt K 132 rs.

Shape armhole
C.off 10 sts beg next 2 rs.
Cont in stripe patt until RC 236.

Shape shoulder
C.off 30 (38) sts beg next 2 rs.
Rel rem 64 sts on WY.

RIGHT FRONT
Col A, c.on in 1 × 1 rib 63 (61)
sts.
RC 000, T2/2, K 12 rs.
Trans sts to M/bed. Inc 1 st.
RC 000, MT.
Working in stripe patt K 132 rs.

Shape armhole
C.off 10 sts beg next r.
Cont in stripe patt until RC 200.

Shape neck
C.off 10 sts beg next r. K 1 r.
C.off 5 sts beg next r. K 1 r.
Dec 1 st at left beg next & foll alt
rs 9 times in all.
30 (38) sts rem.
Cont to K until RC 236.
C.off rem sts.
Work left front to match rev all
shaping.

SLEEVES
Col A, c.on in 1 × 1 rib 103 (111)
sts.
RC 000, T2/2, K 12 rs.

Trans sts to M/bed. Inc 1 st.
RC 000, MT.
Working in stripe patt K 6 rs.
Inc 1 st both ends next & foll 4th
rs until 128 (136) sts.
Cont to K until RC 66.
Col A only, K 12 rs.
C.off loosely.

NECKBAND
Join shoulder seams.
Col A, c.on in 1 × 1 rib 131 sts.
RC 000, T1/1, K 6 rs. T2/2, K 6 rs.
Trans sts to M/bed.
With wrong side facing pick up
sts evenly around neck.
MT K 1 r. T10, K 1 r.
C.off with latch tool.

FRONT BANDS
(K two)
Col A, c.on in 1 × 1 rib 131 sts.
RC 000, T2/2, K 12 rs.
Trans sts to M/bed.
With wrong side facing pick up
sts evenly along front edge.
MT, K 1 r. T10, K 1 r.
C.off with latch tool.

TO MAKE UP
Press all pieces.
Insert sleeves.
Sew side and sleeve seams.

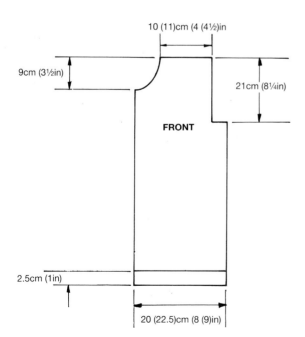

10 (11)cm (4 (4½)in)

9cm (3½in)

21cm (8¼in)

FRONT

2.5cm (1in)

20 (22.5)cm (8 (9)in)

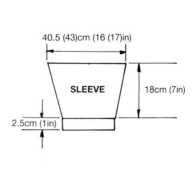

40.5 (43)cm (16 (17)in)

SLEEVE

18cm (7in)

2.5cm (1in)

Saddle shoulder sweater.

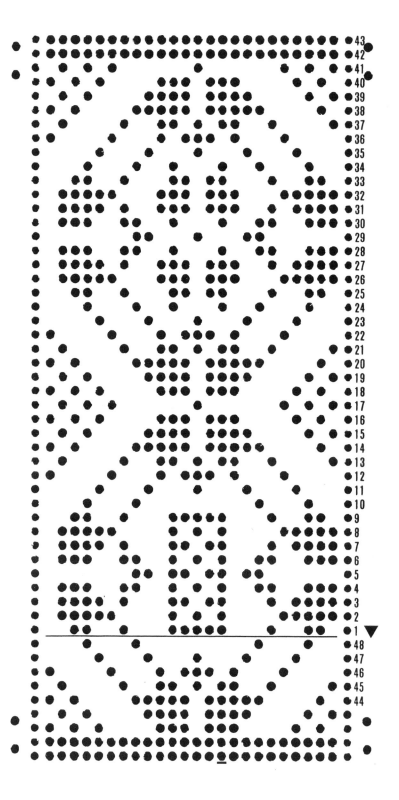

(See photograph on page 56)

Sizes 81 (86, 91, 96, 102, 107, 112)cm (32 (34, 36, 38, 40, 42, 44)in)

Materials 1 cone each BK Charisma cols A & B
Card 10

Tension 28 sts × 40 rs = 10cm (4in)
T at approx 6

BACK
Insert card & lock to K row 1.
Col A, c.on in 1 × 1 rib 119 (125, 133, 139, 147, 153, 161) sts.
RC 000, T2/2, K 30 rs.
Trans sts to M/bed. Inc 1 st.
RC 000, MT.
Rel card & work in fairisle until RC 118 (124, 128, 134, 138, 144, 148).

Shape armholes
RC 000, c.off 7 (8, 8, 8, 8, 8, 9) sts beg next 2 rs.
K 3 rs.
Dec 1 st both ends next & foll 4th rs 13 (13, 14, 15, 16, 17, 18) times in all.
80 (84, 90, 94, 100, 104, 108) sts rem.
K 0 (2, 2, 2, 2, 2, 2) rs.
RC 54 (56, 60, 64, 68, 72, 72).
Dec 1 st both ends next 24 (25, 26, 27, 28, 29, 30) rs.
K 0 (1, 0, 1, 0, 1, 0) rs.
RC 78 (82, 86, 92, 96, 102, 102).
Rel rem 32 (34, 38, 40, 44, 46, 48) sts on WY.

FRONT
K as for back until RC.
44 (44, 48, 52, 54, 58, 58) after armhole shaping.
Cont to dec ev 4th r at sleeve edge as before

At same time
Divide work.
MARK CARD ROW NO.
C.off cent 22 (22, 26, 28, 30, 32, 34) sts.
Place all sts at left in HP or K back onto nylon cord.
Work on right side only.
*Dec 1 st at neck edge next & foll alt rs 5 (6, 6, 6, 7, 7, 7) times in all.
24 (25, 26, 27, 28, 29, 30) sts rem.
RC 54 (56, 60, 64, 68, 72, 72).
Rel work on WY*.
Reset card & complete left side working from * to *.

SLEEVES

Col A, c.on in 1 × 1 rib 59 (61, 63, 65, 67, 69, 71) sts.
RC 000, T2/2, K 30 rs.
Trans sts to M/bed. Inc 1 st.
RC 000, MT. Col A only, K 7 rs.
Inc 1 st both ends next & foll 8th rs until 90 (96, 104, 108, 112, 116, 118) sts.
Cont to K until RC 150 (156, 160, 166, 170, 176, 180).

Shape top

RC 000. C.off 7 (8, 8, 8, 8, 8, 9) sts beg next 2 rs.
Dec 1 st both ends next & foll alt rs until 24 (26, 30, 30, 30, 30, 30) sts rem.
RC 54 (56, 60, 64, 68, 72, 72).
K 34 (36, 36, 38, 38, 40, 40) rs.
RC 88 (92, 96, 102, 106, 112, 112).
C.off.
Join three raglans leaving left back open

NECKBAND

Col A, c.on in 1 × 1 rib 119 (123, 131, 145, 149, 155, 159) sts.
RC 000, T1/1, K 4 rs. T2/2, K 4 rs.
T3/3, K 4 rs. T4/4, K 4 rs.
Trans sts to M/bed.
With wrong side facing pick up sts from sleeve on WY at back sleeve and front neck.
MT, K 1 r. T10, K 1 r.
C.off with latch tool.

TO MAKE UP

Press lightly.
Join 4th raglan.
Sew side & sleeve seams.
Press.

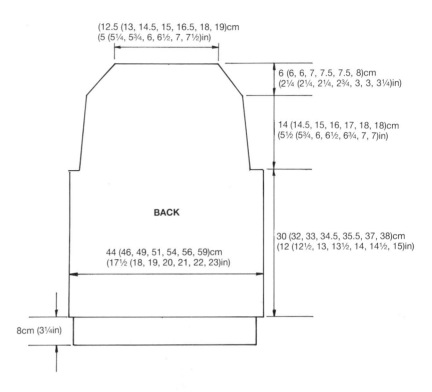

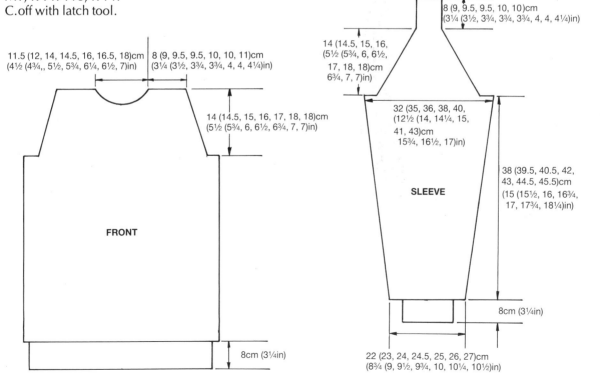

Saddle shoulder sweater—see pattern on page 54

Slash neck sweater.

(See photograph on page 60)

Sizes 81 (86, 91, 97, 102, 107)cm (32 (34, 36, 38, 40, 42)in)

Materials 1 cone each DB Magicolour cols A & B
Card 11

Tension 28 sts × 42 rs = 10cm (4in)
T at approx 7

FRONT & BACK ALIKE
(K two)
Insert card & lock to K row 1.
Col A, c.on in 1 × 1 rib 121 (129, 135, 143, 149, 157) sts.
RC 000, T2/2, K 30 rs.
Trans sts to M/bed. Inc 1 st.
RC 000, MT.
Working in fairisle K 120 (122, 124, 130, 134, 138) rs.
MARK BOTH EDGES
Cont to K until RC 192 (194, 202, 216, 224, 232).
Trans sts to 1 × 1 rib T3/3.
Col A only, K 16 rs.
C.off loosely.

SLEEVES
Insert card & lock to K row 1.
Col A, c.on in 1 × 1 rib 61 (63, 65, 67, 69, 71) sts.
RC 000, T2/2, K 30 rs.
Trans sts to M/bed. Inc 1 st.
RC 000, MT.
Working in fairisle K 2 rs.
Inc 1 st both ends next & foll 4th rs until 106 (108, 118, 126, 128, 130) sts.
Cont to K until RC 138 (144, 148, 154, 158, 160) rs.
C.off loosely.

TO MAKE UP
Join shoulder seams leaving cent open for neck.
Sew side & sleeve seams.
Press with cool iron.

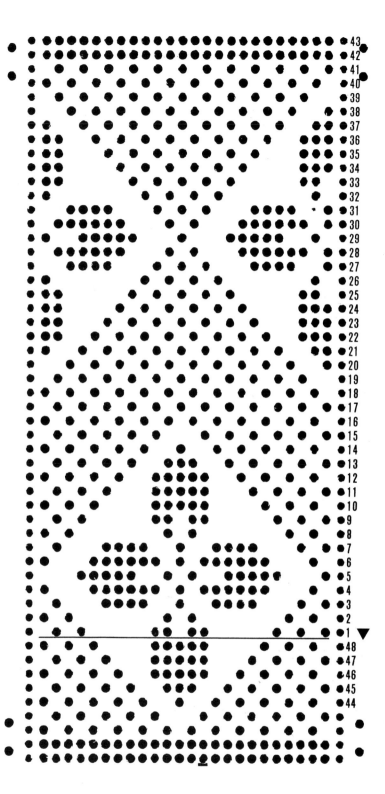

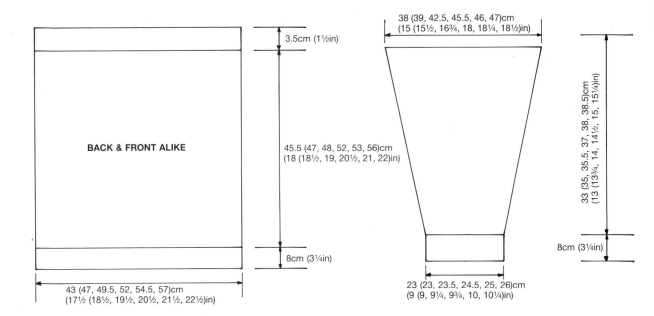

3.5cm (1½in)

45.5 (47, 48, 52, 53, 56)cm
(18 (18½, 19, 20½, 21, 22)in)

8cm (3¼in)

BACK & FRONT ALIKE

43 (47, 49.5, 52, 54.5, 57)cm
(17½ (18½, 19½, 20½, 21½, 22½)in)

38 (39, 42.5, 45.5, 46, 47)cm
(15 (15½, 16¾, 18, 18¼, 18½)in)

33 (35, 35.5, 37, 38, 38.5)cm
(13 (13¾, 14, 14½, 15, 15¼)in)

8cm (3¼in)

23 (23, 23.5, 24.5, 25, 26)cm
(9 (9, 9¼, 9¾, 10, 10¼)in)

Striped batwing.

Sizes 81/91 (97/107)cm (32/36 (38/42)in)

Materials 1 cone DB Magicolour col A
1 cone BK 4-ply Acrylic col B

Tension 32 sts × 44 rs = 10cm (4in)
T at approx 7

BACK
Counting from cent 0 to right c.on in WY 50 (55) sts.
K few rs carr at left.
K 1 r in nylon cord.
Col A, RC 000, MT, K 2 rs.
Inc 1 st at left next & foll alt rs 49 times in all. RC 100.
Cont to inc at left on alt rs.

(See photograph on page 61)

At same time
Col B, K 32 rs.
Col A, cont to inc at left until 120 (125) sts & RC 142.
K 24 (32) rs. MARK LEFT EDGE.
K 8 (24) rs. Col B, K 32 rs.
Col A, K 8 rs.
RC 214 (238) *.

Shape neck
Dec 1 st at right next 10 rs.
K 80 rs. Inc 1 st at right next 10 rs.
K 8 rs. RC 322 (346) **.
Col B, K 32 rs. Col A, K 8 (24) rs. MARK LEFT EDGE.
K 24 (32) rs. RC 386 (434).
Dec 1 st at left next & foll alt rs 5 times in all. RC 396 (444).
Cont to dec 1 st at left on alt rs.

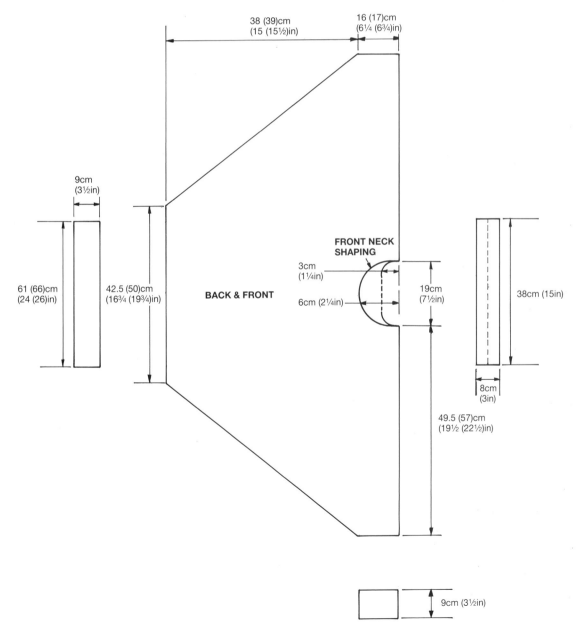

38 (39)cm (15 (15½)in)

16 (17)cm (6¼ (6¾)in)

9cm (3½in)

61 (66)cm (24 (26)in)

42.5 (50)cm (16¾ (19¾)in)

BACK & FRONT

FRONT NECK SHAPING

3cm (1¼in)

6cm (2¼in)

19cm (7½in)

38cm (15in)

8cm (3in)

49.5 (57)cm (19½ (22½)in)

9cm (3½in)

Slash neck sweater—see pattern on page 57

Striped batwing—see pattern on page 59

Col B, K 32 rs. RC 428 (476).
Col A, cont to dec 1 st at left on alt rs until 50 (55) sts rem.
RC 524 (574). K 2 rs.
Rel work on WY.

FRONT

K as for back to *.

Shape neck

Dec 1 st at right next 18 rs.
K 64 rs. Inc 1 st at right next 18 rs.
K 8 rs. RC 322 (346).
Cont as for back from **.

WELTS

(K two)
Col A, c.on in 1 × 1 rib 125 (135) sts.

RC 000, T2/2, K 40 rs.
Trans sts to M/bed.
Pick up sts between markers from front or back waist.
MT, K 1 r. T10, K 1 r.
C.off with latch tool.

CUFFS

(K two)
Col B, c.on in 1 × 1 rib 61 (65) sts.
RC 000, T2/2, K 40 rs.
Trans sts to M/bed.
With wrong side facing pick up sts evenly from sleeve edge.
MT, K 1 r. T10, K 1 r.
C.off with latch tool.

NECKBAND

Col B, c.on in 1 × 1 rib 151 sts.
RC 000, T3/3, K 10 rs. T2/2, K 6 rs.
T10/8, K 1 r. T2/2, K 14 rs.
T3/3, K 2 rs. T5/5, K 1 r.
Trans sts to M/bed.
With wrong side facing pick up sts around neck.
MT, K 1 r. T10, K 1 r.
C.off with latch tool.

TO MAKE UP

Sew top and bottom sleeve seams.
Fold neckband to inside and slip st into pos.
Press with warm iron.

(See photograph on page 64)

Sizes 81 (86, 91, 97, 102)cm (32 (34, 36, 38, 40)in)

Materials 1 cone each Argyll Ferndale cols A & B

Tension 28 sts × 40 rs = 10cm (4in)
T at approx 7

BACK

Col A, c.on in 1 × 1 rib 121 (129, 135, 143, 149) sts.
RC 000, T2/2, K 30 rs.
Trans sts to M/bed. Inc 1 st.
RC 000, MT.
Col B, K 20 rs. Col A, K 20 rs.
Rep from * to * throughout garment.
Cont to K until RC 132 (132, 132, 142, 142).

Shape armholes

C.off 4 (4, 4, 5, 5) sts beg next 2 rs.

Dec 1 st both ends ev r until 102 (102, 96, 102, 96) sts rem.
Dec 1 st both ends next & foll alt rs until 86 (90, 90, 94, 94) sts rem**.
Cont to K until RC 208 (208, 208, 218, 218).

Shape shoulders

C.off 11 (11, 11, 12, 12) sts beg next 4 rs.
Rel rem 48 (48, 48, 50, 50) sts on WY.

FRONT

K as for back to **.
Cont to K until RC 174.

Shape neck

Push 54 (56, 56, 58, 58) sts at left into HP or K back onto nylon cord.
Dec 1 st at neck next & foll alt rs until 22 (22, 22, 24, 24) sts rem.
Cont to K until RC 208 (208, 208, 218, 218).

Shape shoulder

C.off 11 (11, 11, 12, 12) sts beg next & foll alt r. K 1 r.
Leave cent 14 sts in HP or on nylon cord & work left side to match rev shaping.
Rel cent sts on WY.

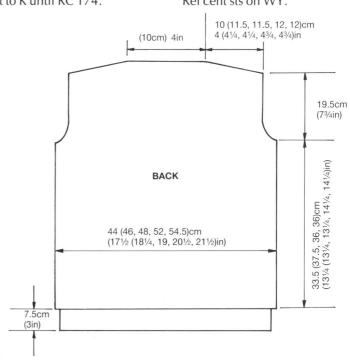

10 (11.5, 11.5, 12, 12)cm
4 (4¼, 4¼, 4¾, 4¾)in

(10cm) 4in

19.5cm
(7¾in)

BACK

44 (46, 48, 52, 54.5)cm
(17½ (18¼, 19, 20½, 21½)in)

33.5 (37.5, 36, 36)cm
(13¼ (13¼, 13¼, 14¼, 14¼)in)

7.5cm
(3in)

SLEEVES

Col A, c.on in 1 × 1 rib 55 (55, 55, 59, 59) sts.
RC 000, T2/2, K 30 rs.
Trans sts to M/bed. Inc 1 st.
RC 000.
Working in stripe patt K 7 rs.
Inc 1 st both ends next & foll 6th rs until 86 (90, 90, 94, 94) sts.
Cont to K until RC 132 (132, 132, 142, 142).

Shape top

C.off 4 (4, 4, 5, 5) sts beg next 2 rs. K 3 rs.
Dec 1 st both ends next & foll 4th rs until 74 (82, 82, 82, 82) sts rem.
Dec 1st both ends next & foll alt rs 2 (0, 0, 0, 1) times.
28 sts rem.
C.off.

NECKBAND

Join right shoulder seam.
Col A, c.on in 1 × 1 rib 119 sts.
RC 000, T3/3, K 4 rs. T2/2, K 4 rs.
T1/1, K 4 rs. T4/4, K 1 r.
T1/1, K 4 rs. T2/2, K 4 rs.
T3/3, K 4 rs.
Trans sts to M/bed.
With wrong side facing pick up sts around neck.
MT, K 1 r. T10, K 1 r.
C.off with latch tool.

TO MAKE UP

Press each piece lightly.
Join left shoulder seam.
Insert sleeves.
Sew side & sleeve seams.
Fold neckband to inside & slip st into pos.
Press.

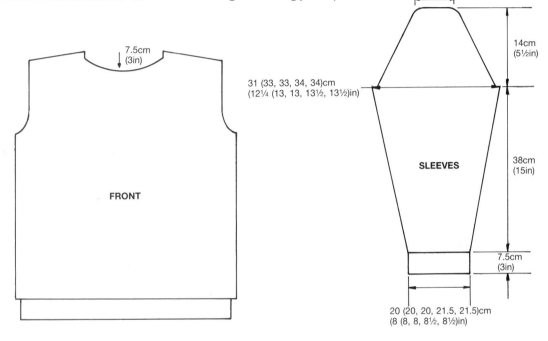

7.5cm (3in)

FRONT

31 (33, 33, 34, 34)cm (12¼ (13, 13, 13½, 13½)in)

10cm (4in)

14cm (5½in)

SLEEVES

38cm (15in)

7.5cm (3in)

20 (20, 20, 21.5, 21.5)cm (8 (8, 8, 8½, 8½)in)

Striped sweater—see pattern on page 62

Lace & Weaving batwing sweater.

(See photograph on page 68)

Sizes 81/86 (97/107)cm (32/36 (38/40)in)

Materials 1 cone Argyll Starlite col A
2 balls Argyll Mistral col B
Cards 12 and 13

Tension 22 sts × 36 rs = 10cm (4in) over weaving patt
T at approx 10
T7 over lace patt

Note Purl side is right side of garment

BACK or FRONT
(K two)
Insert card 12 & lock to K row 1.
Working from cent 0 to right, c.on in WY. 40 (50) sts.
K few rs carr at left.
K 1 r in nylon cord.
Weight work:
Col A, RC 000, MT, K 2 rs.
Working in lace, inc 1 st at left next & foll alt rs 66 times in all.
RC 134.
MARK LEFT EDGE.
K 20 (30) rs. Insert card 13.
Col A in feeder 1, col B weaving yarn work in woven patt until RC 176 (186).

Shape neck
Dec 1 st at right next & foll alt rs 4 times in all. K 60 rs.
Inc 1 st at right next & foll alt rs 4 times in all.
RC 252 (262). K 22 rs.
MARK LEFT EDGE.
Insert card 12.
Working in lace patt, col A only, K 20 (30) rs.
Dec 1 st at left next & foll alt rs 66 times in all until 40 (50) sts rem.
K 2 rs. Rel work on WY.

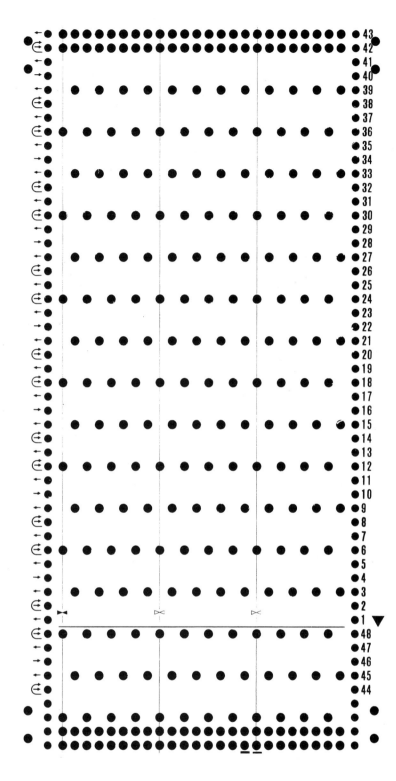

Above: card 12

WELTS

(K two)
Col A, c.on in 1 × 1 rib 129 (139) sts.
RC 000, T2/2, K 46 rs.
Trans sts to M/bed.
With wrong side facing pick up sts evenly around front or back waist.
T6, K 1 r. T10, K 1 r.
C.off with latch tool.

CUFFS

(K two)
Col A, c.on in 1 × 1 rib 63 (67) sts.
RC 000, T2/2, K 46 rs.
Trans sts to M/bed.
With wrong side facing pick up sts evenly around sleeve edge.
T6, K 1 r. T10, K 1 r.
C.off with latch tool.

NECKBAND

Col A, c.on in 1 × 1 rib 171 sts.
RC 000, T3/3, K 15 rs. T10/8, K 1 r.
T3/3, K 14 rs. T10/8, K 1 r.
C.off with latch tool.

TO MAKE UP

Join inside & outside sleeve seams.
Fold neck band to inside & slip st into pos.
Press with cool iron.

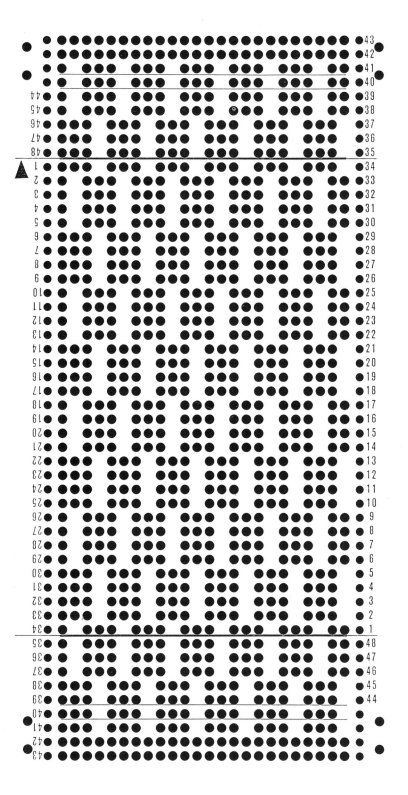

Above: card 13

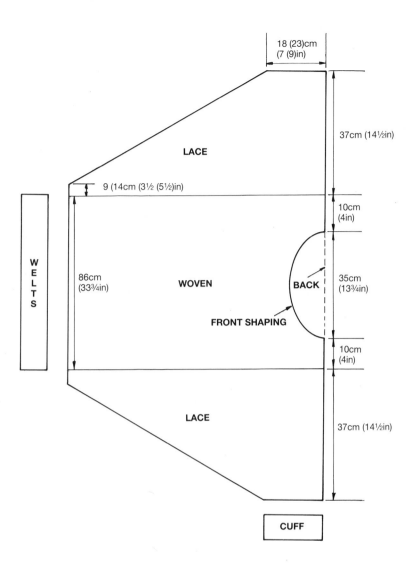

18 (23)cm
(7 (9)in)

37cm (14½in)

LACE

9 (14cm (3½ (5½)in)

10cm
(4in)

WELTS

86cm
(33¾in)

WOVEN

BACK

35cm
(13¾in)

FRONT SHAPING

10cm
(4in)

LACE

37cm (14½in)

CUFF

Lace and weaving batwing sweater—see pattern on page 65

Woven fringed top suit—see pattern on page 70

(See photograph on page 69)

Sizes 86/97cm (34/38in)

Materials 3 × 250gm cones of
fine fleck tweed col A
1 × 250gm mercerised cotton
col B
1 × 100gm hank of chunky tweed
col C
1 × 100gm hank of aran wool
col D
1 × 100gm hank of aran wool
(natural) col E
All yarns are available from
Rowan yarns
elastic to fit waist
Card 14

Tension Top—26 sts × 46
rs = 10cm (4in) over weaving patt
T at approx 7.
Skirt—31 sts × 40 rs = 10cm (4in)
over SS
T at approx 7.

Note Weaving pattern—Set
mach to 'weave' throughout.
Bring end n nearest carr forward
beg of each row to catch weaving
yarn in.
Patt rep 24 sts × 24 rs.
*Col B weave col D K 1 r.
Col B weave col C K 1 r.
Col A K 6 rs.
Col B weave col E K 6 rs.
Col A K 6 rs ***.
Col B weave col C K 1 r.
Col B weave col D K 1 r.
Col B K 2 rs*.

FRONT
Insert card & lock to K row 1.
Col B, c.on by hand ns 1—40 right
of cent 0.
Carr at right MT, K 2 rs.
Rel card work in weaving patt
throughout.
RC 000, MT, K 2 rs.
Col. A, c.on 36 sts at right, K

13 rs. RC 15.
Col A,c.on 78 sts at left, K 10 rs.
RC 25.
Inc 1 st at left beg next & ev foll
10th rs 6 times in all. 160 sts.
Cont to K until RC 93.

Shape Neck
*C.off 4 sts beg next r. K 1 r.
C.off 2 sts beg next & foll alt r.
K 1 r.

Dec 1 st beg next & ev foll alt rs 4
times in all. K 1 r. RC 107.
Dec 1 st beg next & foll 4th r.
K 3 rs.
Dec 1 st beg next r.
Cont to K until RC 147.
Inc 1 st beg next & foll 4th r. K 3
rs. RC 155.
Inc 1 st beg next & ev foll alt r 5
times in all. K 1 r. RC 165.

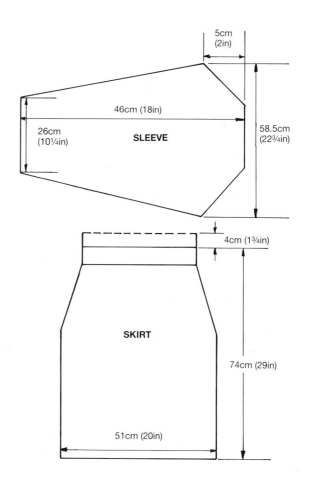

C.on 2 sts beg next & foll alt r.
K 1 r.
C.on 4 sts beg next r. K 1 r. RC
171.
** K 10 rs. RC 181.
Dec 1 st beg next & foll 10th r 6
times in all.
Cont to K until RC 247.
C.off 78 sts loosely at left. K 13 rs.
RC 260.
C.off 36 sts loosely at right. K 2 rs.
Col B, K 1 r.
C. off loosely.

BACK
K as for front to *.
C.off 2 sts beg next r. K 1 r.
RC 95.
Dec 1 st beg next r. K 1 r.
Dec 1 st beg next r.
Cont to K until RC 165.
Inc 1 st beg next & foll alt r. K 1 r.
C.on 2 sts beg next r. K 1 r.
RC 171.
K as for front from **.

SLEEVES
Insert card & lock to K row 16.
Col A, c.on 58 sts left cent 0, 50
sts right cent 0 by hand. 108 sts.
Carr at right, K 2 rs.
Mark 14th st from right edge.
RC 000. Leave 20 ns at right in
WP. Push rest into HP. K 2 rs.
Always taking yarn round last n in
HP, push 3 ns at left to WP next &
ev foll alt rs until RC 46.
At same time Inc 1 st at right beg
next & ev foll 6th r.
Push 2 ns at left into WP next &
foll alt rs until all ns in WP.
Cont to inc 1 st at right side ev 6th
rs until 122 sts.
Cont to K until RC 112.
Rel card working in weaving patt
starting from *** K 30 rs.
Col A, cont to K until RC 170.
Carr at right.
Dec 1 st beg next & ev foll 6th r
until RC 188.
Working from left, push 1 st into
HP ev r until RC 210.
At same time Push 1 st into HP
next & foll 6th rs at right.
Working from left, push 2 sts into
HP next r.
Push 1 st into HP next r.
Rep last 2 rs until RC 254.
Cont to dec 1 st ev 6th r at right.
K 1 r across all ns.
Mark 14th st from right.
C.off loosely.

FINISH FABRIC
Neaten all edges.
Block all pieces to size.
Cut away long floats of col E as
folls.
'SHORT FRINGES'—cut close to
fabric top & bottom.
'LONG FRINGES'—cut close to
bottom only allowing fringes to
hang down.

There are 11 woven bands of col
E across body.
Counting down from shoulder cut
the foll number of long fringes on
each band: 0 0 1 2 3 4 3 2 1 0 0.
Cut all other fringes short.
Press with damp cloth.

FRONT & BACK HEMS
(K two)

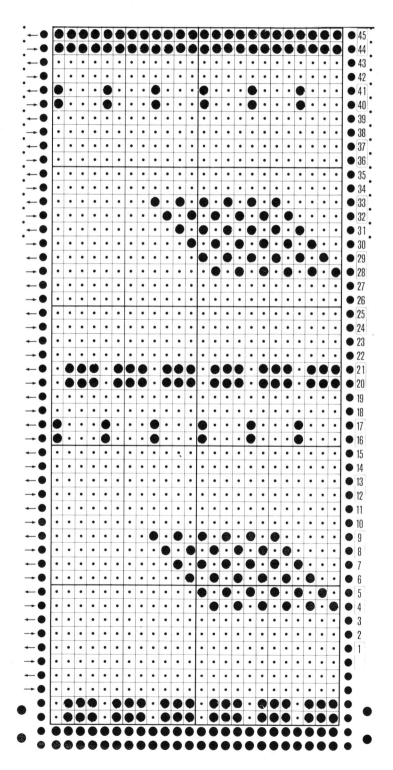

Bring forward 140 ns.
With wrong side facing pick up sts from front or back bottom edge.
*Bring all ns forward taking sts behind latches.
Carr at right.
Col B, MT, K 1 r. T10, K 1 r.
Col A, MT-1, K 4 rs. MT + 1, K 1 r. MT-1, K 5 rs.
Turn up hem picking up loops from T10, col B row.
T10, K 2 rs. C.off with latch tool*.

SIDE OPENING HEMS

(K four)
Bring forward 40 ns.
With wrong side facing pick up sts from side opening.
Work as for front & back hems from * to *.

SLEEVE HEMS

(K two)
Bring forward 70 ns.
With wrong side facing pick up sts from sleeve edges.
Work as for front & back hems from * to *.

NECKBAND

Join shoulder seams.
Bring forward 114 ns.
With right side facing pick up sts around neck.
Carr at right.
Col B, MT, K 1 r.
Col A, MT, K 2 rs. MT-1, K 1 r.

MT-2, K 1 r. MT-3, K 1 r. MT, K 1 r. MT-3, K 1 r. MT-2, K 1 r. MT-1, K 1 r. MT, K 3 rs.
Col B, MT + 1, K 1 r.
Rel work on WY.

TO MAKE UP

Join shoulder seam.
Finish hems by inserting a knitting needle and pulling down on loose tension row.
Sew side & sleeve seams.
At side seams overlap front hems over back. Press all seams.

SKIRT

(K two pieces)
Col A, c.on in 1 + 1 rib 176 sts.
T2/2, K 3 rs circular.
T3/3, K 4 rs.
Trans ev 4th st on ribber bed to M-bed.
Bring all empty ns on M/bed to WP.
**** 111.111.111.111.
.1...1...1...1
Take loop from base of oppos st on ribber bed onto empty n on M/bed (except end right n). At left, trans end st from M/bed to ribber bed.
At right, trans end st onto adjacent n on ribber bed.
Set pitch lever to H (to adjust length of skirt plus or minus 20 rows per inch in this section)

Use side weights & 3 claw weights across fabric—keep moving weights up regularly.
MT-1/1, K 190 rs.
Set pitch lever to P.
Trans ev 4th st on M/bed onto adjacent left n to give n arrangement as ****
At right, trans end st on M/bed onto adjacent n.
MT-1/2, K 80 rs.
Trans ev 4th st from M/bed to ribber bed for 1 + 1 rib.
At right & left, trans end st from ribber bed to M/bed.
MT-3/3, K 28rs
Turn racking handle 1 pos.
Trans all sts from ribber bed to ns in WP on M/bed
Remove ribber arm drop ribber bed.
Work on M/bed only bring all ns forward so that sts go behind latches.
MT-3, K 1 r.
Rel work on WY.

TO MAKE UP

Block & press with damp cloth.
Turn waistband onto right side & backstitch through open loops.
Sew side seams.
Thread elastic through waist.
Steam press.

Tuck stitch suit.

Sizes 81/86 (91/97)cm (32/34 (36/38)in)

Materials 2 cones BK Shimmer, col A
1 cone BK Shimmer, col B
cards 15 and 16
8 buttons
elastic to fit waist

Tension 30 sts × 80 rs = 10cm (4in) over single end tuck st patt T at approx 3.

Note Purl side is right side of garment

Top

FRONT

Insert card 15 & lock to K row 1.
C.on in WY 130 (140) sts.
K few rs. Carr at right.
Col A, RC 000, T2, K 11 rs.
T9, K 1 R. T2, K 11 rs.
Turn up hem.
T8, K 1 r. MT.
Rel card & work in tuck patt until RC 220

Shape Armholes
C.off 8 sts beg next 2 rs.

(See photograph on page 76)

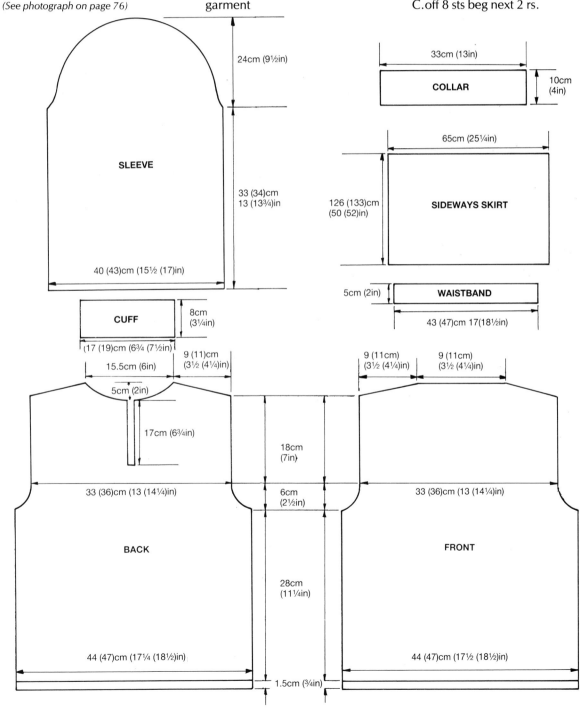

SLEEVE

24cm (9½in)

33 (34)cm 13 (13¾)in

40 (43)cm (15½ (17)in)

CUFF

8cm (3¼in)

(17 (19)cm (6¾ (7½)in)

COLLAR 33cm (13in) 10cm (4in)

SIDEWAYS SKIRT 65cm (25¼in) 126 (133)cm (50 (52)in)

WAISTBAND 5cm (2in) 43 (47)cm 17(18½)in

15.5cm (6in)

9 (11)cm (3½ (4¼)in)

9 (11cm) (3½ (4¼)in)

9 (11cm) (3½ (4¼)in)

5cm (2in)

17cm (6¾in)

18cm (7in)

6cm (2½in)

BACK 33 (36)cm (13 (14¼)in)

FRONT 33 (36)cm (13 (14¼)in)

28cm (11¼in)

44 (47)cm (17¼ (18½)in)

44 (47)cm (17½ (18½)in)

1.5cm (¾in)

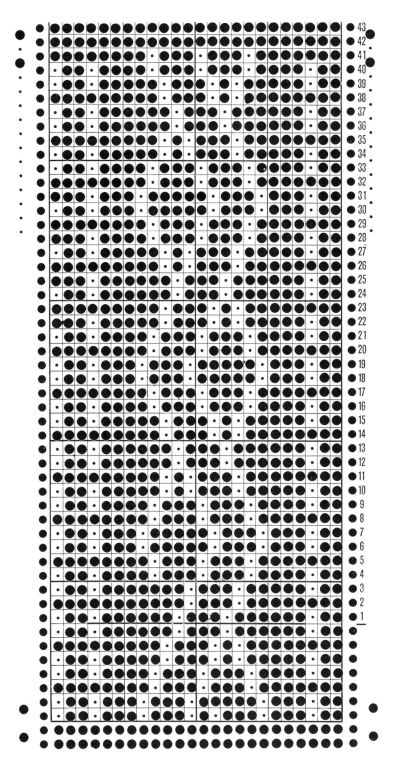

Above: card 15

C.off 2 sts beg next 4 rs.
Dec 1 st beg next 6 rs *.
100 (110) sts rem.
Cont to K until RC 360.

Shape Shoulder

C.off 9 (10) sts beg next 4 rs.
C.off 9 (12) sts beg next 2 rs.
Rel work on WY.

BACK

K as for front to *.
Divide for back opening.
C.off cent 4 sts.
Place all ns at left into HP or K
back onto nylon cord.
MARK CARD ROW NO.
Cont to K on right side only until
RC 349.

Shape Neck

C.off 13 sts beg next r.
Dec 1 st at neck edge next 6 rs.
K 4 rs.

Shape Shoulder

C.off 9 (10) sts beg next & foll alt
r. K 1 r.
C.off 9 (12) sts beg next r.
Work left side to match rev
shaping.

SLEEVES

Insert card 15 & lock to K row 1.
C.on in WY 120 (128) sts.
K few rs. Carr at right.
Col A, RC 000, MT.
Rel card & work in tuck patt until
RC 260 (270).

Shape Top

C.off 8 sts beg next 2 rs.
C.off 1 (2) sts both ends next &
foll 4th rs.
8 times in all.
Dec 1 st both ends next & foll 4th
rs until 80 sts rem. RC 307, K 3 rs.
C.off 2 sts beg next 2 rs. K 3 rs.
Cont to dec from * to * until 40 sts
rem.
SS, K 1 r. RC 360
C.off.

CUFFS

(K two)
Bring forward 60 (64) ns.
With wrong side facing pick up
sts from sleeve placing 2 sts on
each n.
RC 000, MT, K 10 rs. MT-1, K
20 rs.
MT-2, K 9 rs. T8, K 1 r. MT-2, K
9 rs.
MT-1, K 20 rs. MT, K 10 rs. T10,
K 1 r.
C.off with latch tool.

COLLAR

Using 1 end col A & 1 end col B
insert card 15 & lock to K row 1.
Bring forward 100 ns.
With right side facing pick up sts
evenly from front & back.
Rel card & work in tuck until
RC 60.
C.off with latch tool.

FRONT BAND

Bring forward 63 ns.
With wrong side facing pick up
sts evenly along left front.
RC 000, MT-1, K 10 rs. T9, K 1 r.
MT-1, K 10 rs. T10, K 1 r.
C.off with latch tool.

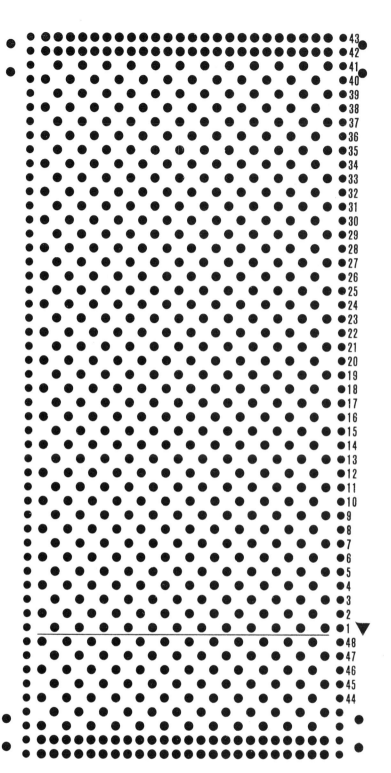

Above: card 16

end col B)
Insert card 16 and lock to K row 1.
C.on in WY 150 sts.
K few rs ending with carr at left.
K in nylon cord.
Col A, RC 000, rel card.
T4 & *work in tuck st. K 20 rs
Col B, T3, K 10 rs in SS*.
Rep from * to * until 33 (35) stripe patterns have been worked.
Join back seam.
Pick up sts above nylon cord.
Mt + 1, K 1 r. T10 K 1 r.
C.off with latch tool.

WAISTBAND

(K two)
Bring forward 128 (138) ns.
With wrong side facing pick up sts from front or back skirt.
Using 2 ends col A, MT, K 19 rs.
T9, K 1 r.
MT, K 19 rs. T10, K 1 r.
C.off with latch tool.

FINISH FABRIC

To give curved hem, at waist edge where col B joins col A, pull col B threads to give a tight r.

TO MAKE UP

Slip st waistband to inside.
Thread elastic through waist.
Press with steam iron.

BUTTONBAND

K as for front band working 8 buttonholes evenly along 5th & 14th rs.

TO MAKE UP

Steam press each piece.
Join shoulder seams.
Set in sleeves.
Sew side & sleeve seams.
Fold cuffs & front bands to inside & slip st into pos.
Sew on buttons.
Press.

Skirt

NOTE Pattern (K 20 rs tuck st with 2 ends col A and K 10 rs SS with 1

Tuck stitch suit—see pattern on page 73

Mock rib suit—see pattern on page 78

Mock rib suit.

(See photograph on page 77)

Sizes 81/86 (91/97)cm (32/34 (36/38)in)

Materials 2 cones BK Charade, col A
Cotton thread, col B
Elastic to fit waist

Tension 32 sts × 44 rs = 10cm (4in)
T at approx 5.

Top

BACK & FRONT ALIKE

Col A throughout, bring forward 153 (161) sts. Arrange in 5 × 3 rib.
C. on in WY. K few rs.
Carr at left. K 1 r in nylon cord.
RC 000, MT-1, K 12 rs. T9, K 1 r.
MT-1, K 12 rs. Turn up hem. T9, K 1 r.
RC 000, MT, K 120 rs.
MARK BOTH EDGES
Cont to K until RC 200 rs.
Bring forward the cent n of those in NWP. K 1 r.
Bring forward empty ns.
Cont to K until RC 220.
C.off 30 (34) sts beg next 2 rs.
C.off rem sts.
Join shoulder seams.

SLEEVES

Bring forward 125 ns in 5 × 3 rib.
With right side facing pick up sts between armhole markers.
RC 000, MT, K 160 rs.
Rel work on WY.

CUFFS

(K two)
Bring forward 60 ns.
With knit side facing pick up sts from sleeve edge gathering evenly.
RC 000, MT-1, K 7 rs. T9, K 1 r.
MT-1, K 7 rs. T10, K 1 r.
C.off with latch tool

TO MAKE UP

Press all pieces. Sew side & sleeve seams. Fold cuff band to inside & slip st into pos.
Press.

Skirt

C.on in WY 180 sts. K few rs.
Carr at right.
Col A, RC 000, MT, K 4 rs.
Carr at right.
*Always taking yarn round last n in HP at oppos end to carr, push 25 sts into HP next & foll alt rs 6 times in all. K 1 r.
Push all ns back into WP.
Col B, K 2 rs.
Col A, push 150 ns at left back into HP next r. K 1 r.
Push 25 sts at right into WP next & foll alt rs 6 times in all**.
K 10 rs*.
Rep from * to * 28 (30) times.
Rep from * to ** once. K 5 rs.
Join back seam.
Pick up sts above WY.
MT + 1, K 1 r. T9, K 1 r.
C.off with latch tool.

WAISTBAND

(K two)
Bring forward 120 (130) ns.
With right side facing pick up sts from front or back skirt.
RC 000, MT-1, K 17 rs. T9, K 1 r.
MT-1, K 17 rs. T10, K 1 r.
C.off with latch tool.

TO MAKE UP

Steam press. Fold waistband to inside & slip st into pos.
Thread elastic through waist.
Press.

Note Needle setting for top:

111		111		111		111	— NWP
111	11111		11111		11111	111	— WP

3 sts at both ends in WP

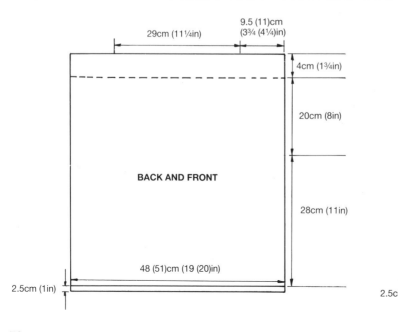

9.5 (11)cm (3¾ (4¼)in)
29cm (11¼in)
4cm (1¾in)
20cm (8in)
28cm (11in)
BACK AND FRONT
48 (51)cm (19 (20)in)
2.5cm (1in)

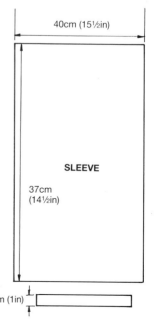

40cm (15½in)
SLEEVE
37cm (14½in)
2.5cm (1in)

Tweedknit suit.

Sizes 81 (86, 91, 97, 102)cm (32 (34, 36, 38, 40)in)

Materials 2 cones Bramwell Tweedknit col A
1 cone Bramwell Hobby col B
Elastic to fit waist

Tension 28 sts × 40 rs = 10cm (4in)
T at approx 7

Note Purl side is used as right side of garment

Skirt

C.on in WY 180 sts.
K few rs. Carr at right.
Bring all ns into HP.
Col A, c.on by hand over all ns.
MT, K 4 rs.
*Always taking yarn round last ns in HP at oppos end to carr, RC 000, push 25 sts into HP next & foll alt rs 6 times in all.
K 1 r. RC 12.
Col B, K 2 rs across all ns.
Col A, push 150 ns at left back into HP beg next r.
Push 25 sts at right into WP next & foll alt rs 6 times in all *.
K 10rs**. RC 36.
Rep from * to ** 23 (24, 25, 26, 27) times.
Rep from * to * once.
K 6 rs.
C.off loosely.

WAISTBAND

Bring forward 120 (126, 130, 136, 140) ns.
With knit side facing pick up sts evenly from front or back skirt.
RC 000, MT-1, K 15 rs. T9, K 1 r.
MT-1, K 15 rs. T10, K 1 r.
C.off with latch tool.

TO MAKE UP

Steam press. Fold waistband to inside on fold line.
Join back seam.
Sew waistband into pos.
Thread elastic through waist.
Press.

Top

BACK

Col A, c.on in 1 × 1 rib 121 (129, 135, 143, 149) sts.
RC 000, T1/1, K 30 rs.
Trans sts to M/bed. Inc 1 st.

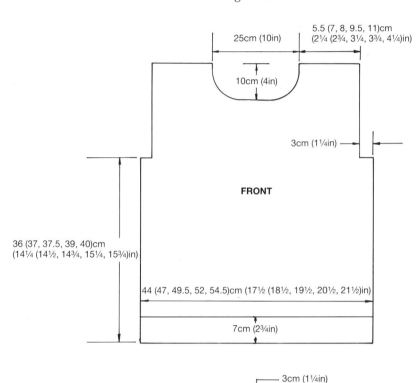

25cm (10in)

5.5 (7, 8, 9.5, 11)cm (2¼ (2¾, 3¼, 3¾, 4¼)in)

10cm (4in)

3cm (1¼in)

FRONT

36 (37, 37.5, 39, 40)cm (14¼ (14½, 14¾, 15¼, 15¾)in)

44 (47, 49.5, 52, 54.5)cm (17½ (18½, 19½, 20½, 21½)in)

7cm (2¾in)

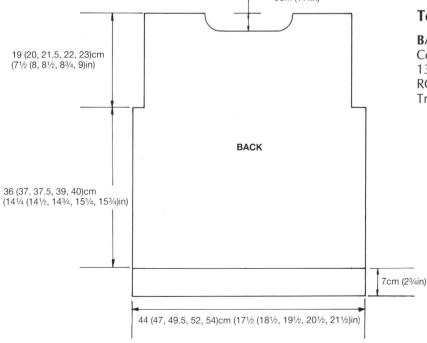

3cm (1¼in)

19 (20, 21.5, 22, 23)cm (7½ (8, 8½, 8¾, 9)in)

BACK

36 (37, 37.5, 39, 40)cm (14¼ (14½, 14¾, 15¼, 15¾)in)

7cm (2¾in)

44 (47, 49.5, 52, 54)cm (17½ (18½, 19½, 20½, 21½)in)

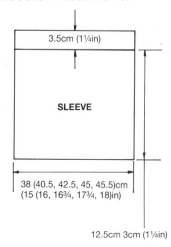

3.5cm (1¼in)

SLEEVE

38 (40.5, 42.5, 45, 45.5)cm (15 (16, 16¾, 17¾, 18)in)

12.5cm 3cm (1¼in)

Tweedknit suit—see pattern on page 79

Short sleeved suit—see pattern on page 83

Col A, RC 000, MT, K 144 (146, 148, 154, 158) rs.

Shape armholes

C.off 10 sts beg next 2 rs *.
Cont to K until RC 208 (214, 220, 230, 236).

Shape neck

Push 66 (70, 73, 77, 80) sts at left into HP or K back onto nylon cord.
Work on right side only.
Always taking yarn round last ns in HP at oppos end to carr push 5 sts at neck into HP next & foll alt rs 4 times in all.
16 (20, 23, 27, 30) sts rem.
Cont to K until RC 220 (226, 232, 242, 248).

Shape shoulder

C.off 5 (6, 8, 9, 10) sts beg next & foll alt r. K 1 r.
C.off 6 (8, 7, 9, 10) sts.
Leave cent 30 sts in HP.
Work left side to match.

Rel cent sts on WY.

FRONT

K as for back to *.
Cont to K until RC 180 (186, 192, 202, 208).

Shape neck

Push 66 (70, 73, 77, 80) sts at left into HP or K back onto nylon cord.
Work on right side only.
Always taking yarn round last ns in HP at oppos end to carr push 5 sts into HP next & foll alt rs 4 times in all.
16 (20, 23, 27, 30) sts rem.
Cont to K until RC 220 (226, 242, 248).

Shape shoulder

C.off 5 (6, 8, 9, 10) sts beg next & foll alt r. K 1 r.
C.off rem 6 (8, 7, 9, 10) sts.
Leave cent 30 sts in HP.
Work left side to match.
Rel cent sts on WY.

SLEEVES

Col A, c.on by hand 106 (112, 118, 124, 126) sts.
RC 000, MT, K 50 rs.
Col B used two ends, K 14 rs.
C.off loosely.

NECKBAND

Bring forward 162 ns.
With knit side facing pick up sts evenly around neck.
RC 000, MT, K 10 rs. MT + 1, K 6 rs.
T10, K 1 r.
C.off loosely.

TO MAKE UP

Press pieces—do not press sleeves edges or neckband.
Join shoulder seams.
Insert sleeves sewing col B to c.off sts.
Sew side & sleeve seams.
Allow sleeve and neck edges to roll.

Short sleeved suit.

(See photograph on page 81)

Sizes 81/86 (91/97)cm (32/34 (36/38)in)

Materials 2 cones BK Charade col A
1 cone BK Shimmer col B
Elastic to fit waist

Tension 32 sts × 44 rs = 10cm (4in)
T at approx 5

Skirt

WY, c.on 180 sts.
K few rs. Carr at right.
Col A, K 6 rs. RC 000.
* Always taking yarn round last n in HP at oppos end to carr, push 15 sts at right into HP next & foll alt rs 10 times in all. K 1 r.
Col B, RC 20, K 2 rs across all ns.
Bring 150 ns at left back into HP.
Push 15 sts at right back into WP next & foll alt rs 10 times in all *.
RC 42, K 10 rs **.
Rep from * to ** 28 (30) times.
Rep from * to * once. K 4 rs.
Rel work on WY.

WAISTBAND
(K two)
Bring forward 124 (134) ns.
With wrong side of work facing pick up sts evenly from front or back waist.
RC 000, MT-1, K 17 rs. T9, K 1 r.
MT-1 K 17 rs. T10, K 1 r.
C.off with latch tool.

TO MAKE UP
Press.
Bring forward 180 ns.
With knit sides together put back seams back onto ns.
MT-1, K 1 r. T10, K 1 r.
C.off with latch tool.
Fold waistband to inside & slip st into pos.

Thread elastic through waist.

Top
BACK
Col A, c.on in 2 × 2 rib 106 (110) sts.
RC 000, T2/2, K 80 rs.
Trans sts to M/bed.
Col B used two ends, MT.
Inc 1 st both ends next & foll 4th rs until 128 (134) sts.
Cont to K until RC 160 **.

Shape armholes
C.off 4 sts beg next 2 rs.
C.off 2 sts beg next 4 rs.
Dec 1 st both ends next r. K 1 r.
Cont to K until RC 246.

Shape shoulders
C.off 26 (29) sts beg next 2 rs.
Rel cent 58 sts on WY.

FRONT
K as for back to **. RC 160.
Cont to K until RC 206.

Shape neck
Push 64 (67) ns at left into HP or K back onto nylon cord.
Work on right side only.
Always taking yarn round last ns in HP at oppos end to carr push 3 sts into HP next & foll alt rs 4 times in all. K 1 r.
Push 2 sts into HP next & foll alt rs 4 times in all until 26 (29) sts rem.
Cont to K until RC 246.
C.off rem sts.
Leave cent 18 sts in HP.
Work left side to match.
Rel cent sts on WY.

SLEEVES
Col A, c.on in 2 × 2 rib 116 sts.
RC 000, T3/3, K 10 rs.
Trans sts to M/bed.
Col B used two ends, RC 000, MT, K 2 rs.
Inc 1 st both ends next & foll alt rs 10 times in all. 136 sts.
Cont to K until RC 46.

Shape top
C.off 4 sts beg next 2 rs.
C.off 2 sts beg next 4 rs.
Dec 1 st both ends next & foll alt rs 30 times in all.
C.off 2 sts beg ev r until 40 sts rem.
C.off.

NECKBAND
Col A, c.on in 2 × 2 rib 144 sts.
RC 000, T4/4, K 6 rs. T3/3, K 2 rs.
T2/2, K 2 rs. T1/1, K 14 rs.

T2/2, K 2 rs. T3/3, K 2 rs.
T4/4, K 6 rs. RC 34.
Trans sts to M/bed.
With knit side facing pick up sts evenly around neck – back 58, front shaping 34, across cent 18, up front shaping 34.
MT, K 1 r. T10, K 1 r.
C.off with latch tool.

TO MAKE UP
Press all pieces with warm iron.
Join shoulder seams.
Insert sleeves.
Sew side & sleeve seams.
Fold neckband to inside & slip st into pos.
Press.

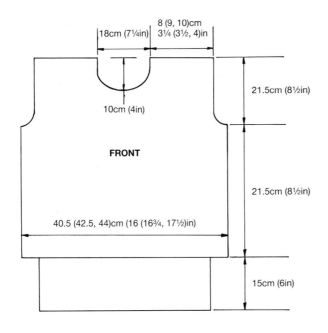

18cm (7¼in)

8 (9, 10)cm
3¼ (3½, 4)in

10cm (4in)

21.5cm (8½in)

FRONT

21.5cm (8½in)

40.5 (42.5, 44)cm (16 (16¾, 17½)in)

15cm (6in)

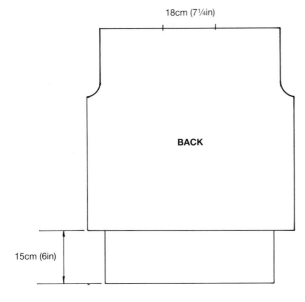

18cm (7¼in)

BACK

15cm (6in)

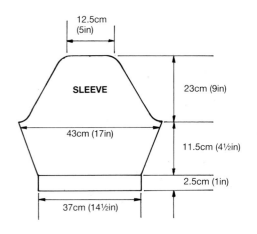

12.5cm (5in)

SLEEVE

23cm (9in)

43cm (17in)

11.5cm (4½in)

2.5cm (1in)

37cm (14½in)

Three piece suit.

(See photograph on page 88)

Sizes 81/86 (91/97, 102/107)cm (32/34 (36/38, 40/42)in)

Materials 1 cone each BK Party Poodle cols A B & C used two ends throughout
Elastic to fit waist

Tension 24 sts × 44 rs = 10cm (4in)
T at approx 8

Jacket

BACK

Col B, c.on in 1 × 1 rib 109 (119, 129) sts.
RC 000, T4/4, K 12 rs.
Trans sts to M/bed. Inc 1 st.
RC 000, MT.
Col B, K 20 rs. Col C, K 20 rs.
*Col A, K 20 rs. Col B, K 4 rs.
Col A, K 20 rs. Col C, K 4 rs*.
Cont to work in stripes from * to * until RC 142 *.

Shape armholes

Keeping stripe patt correct,
c.off 3 (3, 4) sts beg next 4 rs,
c.off 2 (2, 3) sts beg next 4 rs.
Dec 1 st both ends next & foll alt rs until 88 (94, 98) sts rem.
Cont to K until RC 240.

Shape neck & shoulder

Push 52 (55, 57) sts at left into HP or K back onto nylon cord.
Work on right side only.
At same time
dec 1 st at neck next 9 rs & c.off 5 sts beg next & foll alt r. K 1 r.
C.off 5 (6, 7) sts beg next & foll alt r. K 1 r.
C.off 7 (8, 8) sts.
C.off cent 16 sts in HP and work left side to match rev shaping.

RIGHT FRONT

Col B, c.on in 1 × 1 rib 55 (61,

65) sts.
RC 000, T4/4, K 12 rs.
Trans sts to M/bed. Inc 1 st.
RC 000, MT, WORK IN STRIPES as for back until * RC 142.

Shape armhole & neck
At same time
dec 1 st at neck next & foll 4th rs & c.off 3 (3, 4) sts beg next & foll alt r. K 1 r.
C.off 2 (2, 3) sts beg next & foll alt r. K 1.
Dec 1 st at armhole next & foll alt rs 1 (3, 4) times in all.
Cont to dec 1 st at neck ev 4th rs until 27 (30, 32) sts rem.
Cont to K until RC 240.

Shape shoulder

C.off 5 sts beg next & foll alt r. K 1 r.
C.off 5 (6, 7) sts beg next & foll alt r. K 1 r.
C.off rem 7 (8, 8) sts.
Work left front to match rev shaping.

SLEEVES

Col A, c.on in 1 × 1 rib 75 (79, 85) sts.
RC 000, T4/4, K 12 rs.
Trans sts to M/bed. Inc 1 st.
RC 000, MT. Col A, K 2 rs.
Inc 1 st both ends next & foll 6th rs until 92 (98, 104) sts.
At same time
On RC 8, *col C, K 4 rs. Col A, K 20 rs.
Col B, K 4 rs. Col A, K 20 rs*.
Work in stripes from * to * until RC 66.

Shape top

C.off 3 (3, 4) sts beg next 4 rs.
C.off 2 (2, 3) sts beg next 2 rs.
Dec 1 st both ends next & foll 4th rs 10 times in all.
52 (58, 58) sts rem. K 1 r.
Dec 1 st both ends next & foll alt rs until 26 sts rem.
RC 140 (146, 146).
C.off rem sts.
Join shoulder seams.

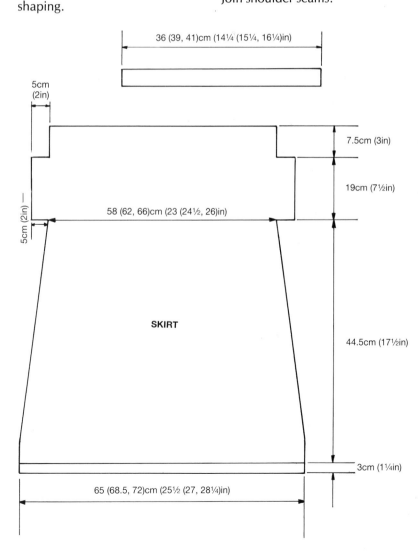

36 (39, 41)cm (14¼ (15¼, 16¼)in)

5cm (2in)

7.5cm (3in)

19cm (7½in)

5cm (2in)

58 (62, 66)cm (23 (24½, 26)in)

SKIRT

44.5cm (17½in)

3cm (1¼in)

65 (68.5, 72)cm (25½ (27, 28¼)in)

FRONT BANDS

(K two)
Col A, c.on 160 sts.
RC 000, MT-1, K, 12 rs. T10, K
1 r. MT-1, K 12 rs.
With wrong side facing pick up
sts along one front to cent back.
MT, K 1 r. T10, K, 1 r.

TO MAKE UP

Insert sleeves.
Sew side & sleeve seams.

Fold front bands to inside & slip st
into pos.
Press lightly.

Camisole Top

(K two)
Col B, c.on in 1 × 1 rib 85 (95,
103) sts.
RC 000, T4/4, K 12 rs.
Trans sts to M/bed. Inc 1 st.
Col B, RC 000, K 20 rs. Col C, K
20 rs.
*Col A, K 20 rs. Col B, K 4 rs.

Col A, K 20 rs. Col C, K 4 rs. *.
Rep stripe patt from * to * until RC
120.

Shape top

C.off 3 (3, 4) sts beg next 4 rs.
C.off 2 (2, 3) sts beg next 4 rs.
Dec 1 st both ends next & foll alt
rs until 78 (84, 88) sts rem.
Cont to K until RC 140.
Cont in col A only, c.on 18 (20,
22) sts beg next 2 rs.
MT-1, K 6 rs. T10, K 1 r.

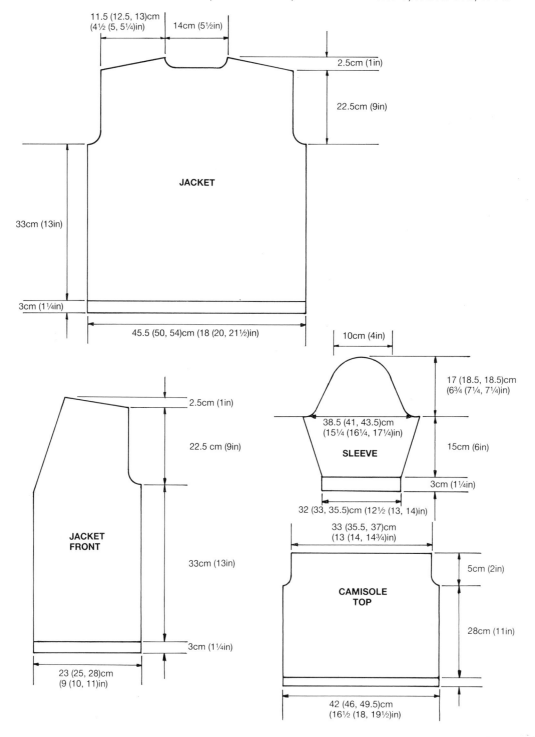

MT-1, K 6 rs.
C.off.

SHOULDER STRAPS
C.on 5 sts.
Work 2 cords long enough to tie over shoulders.

TO MAKE UP
Join side seams & sew c.on sts of band to underarm.
Fold band to inside & slip st into pos.
Press lightly.

Skirt
(K two)
Col B, c.on in 1 × 1 rib 153 (161, 169) sts.
RC 000, T4/4, K 12 rs.

Trans sts to M/bed. Inc 1 st.
Col B, RC 000, K 20 rs.
Col C, dec 1 st both ends next & foll 20th rs 7 times in all
At same time
on RC 40 work in stripe patt from* to *until RC 192.
140 (148, 156) sts.

POCKET FLAPS
C.on 12 sts beg next 2 rs.
Cont to K until RC 274.
C.off 12 sts beg next 2 rs.
Cont to K until RC 308.
Rel work on WY.
Bring forwad 86 (92, 98) ns.
Rehang sts from skirt dec 54 (56, 58) sts evenly across row.
Col A, MT-1, K 20 rs. T10,

K 1 r. MT-1, K 20 rs.
C.off loosely.

POCKET LINING
Col A 1 strand, c.on by hand 100 sts.
RC 000, T3, K 104 rs.
C.off.

TO MAKE UP
Fold pocket linings in half lengthways—sew one side to pocket flap, one side to front side seam. Fold flap to inside.
Sew pocket seams.
Join side seams.
Fold waistband to inside & slip st into pos.
Thread elastic through waist.

Three piece suit—see pattern on page 85

Short sleeved cardi' suit—see pattern on page 90

Short sleeved cardi' suit.

(See photograph on page 89)

Sizes TOP 81/86 (91/97)cm (32/34 (36/38)in)
SKIRT 81cm (32in) length; 91 (102)cm (36 (40)in) hip

Materials 1 cone DB Fantasia col A
1 cone Argyll Cotton col B
Elastic to fit waist
Elastic to fit upper hip loosely

Tension 34 sts × 56 rs = 10cm (4in)
T at approx 3

Skirt

WY, c.on 198 sts.
K few rs. Carr at right.
Col A, RC 000, MT, *K 30 rs.
Always taking yarn round last ns in HP at oppos end to carr push 20 sts at right into HP next & foll alt rs 8 times in all.
38 ns rem in WP.
Push 20 sts into WP next & foll alt rs 8 times in all. RC 62.
Rep from * to * 18 (19) times.
Rel work on WY.

WAISTBAND

Bring forward 150 (170) ns.
With purl side facing pick up sts from front or back waist.
MT, K 20 rs. T8, K 1 r.
MT, K 19 rs. T10, K 1 r.
C.off with latch tool.

TO MAKE UP

Press.
Graft back seam.
Fold waistband to inside & slip st into pos.
Thread elastic through waist.
Give final press.

Top

BACK

Col A, c.on by hand 68 sts right cent 0.
RC 000, MT, K 10 rs.
C.on by hand 110 sts left cent 0.
K 70 (84) rs.
C.on by hand 5 sts at right*.
K 140 rs.
C.off 5 sts at right.
K 70 (84) rs.
C.off 110 sts at left RC 290 (318).
K 10 rs.
C.off rem 68 sts.

FRONT

K as for back to *. K 10 rs.
Work in Intarsia.
Col B, K 9 sts beg next r. K 1 r.
Col B, K 13 sts in beg next r. K 1 r.
Cont to inc 4 sts in Col B next & foll alt rs until 125 sts are in col B. RC 150 (164).
Dec 4 sts in col B next & foll alt rs 29 times until 9 sts in col B.
Dec 9 sts in col B. RC 210 (224).
Col A only, K 10 rs.
C.off 5 sts right. K 70 (84) rs.
C.off 110 sts at left RC 290 (318).
K 10 rs. C.off rem 68 sts.

TO MAKE UP

Press both pieces.
Join shoulder seams.
Fold neck & sleeve edges to inside & slip st into pos.
Turn up 2cm (¾in) at hem & slip st into pos.
Thread elastic through hem.

Jacket

BACK

WY, c.on 170 (186) sts.
K few rs. Carr at right.
K 1 r in nylon cord.
Col B, RC 000, MT, K 14 rs.
MT + 3, K 1 r. MT, K 14 rs.
Turn up hem.
Col A, RC 000, MT, K 180 rs.

Shape armholes

C.off 5 (6) sts beg next 2 rs.
C.off 3 (4) sts beg next 2 rs.
Dec 1 st both ends next & foll alt rs until 152 (168) sts.
Cont to K until RC 300 (306).

Shape shoulder

C.off 6 (7) sts beg next 12 rs.
C.off 6 (8) sts beg next 2 rs.

BACK BAND

Col B, K 14 rs. MT + 3, K 1 r.
MT, K 14 rs. C.off loosely.

LEFT FRONT

WY, c.on 80 (90) sts.
K few rs. Carr at right.
K 1 r in nylon cord.
Col B, RC 000, MT, K 14 rs.
MT + 3, K 1 r.
MT, K 14 rs.
Turn up hem.
Col A, RC 000, MT, K 164 rs.

Shape neck

Dec 1 st at front next & foll 4th rs 34 times.

At same time

On RC 180 shape armhole.
C.off 5 (6) sts beg next r. K 1 r.
C.off 3 (4) sts beg next r. K 1 r.
Dec 1 st beg next & foll alt r.
Cont to dec at front ev 4th r until 42 (50) sts rem.
Cont to K until RC 300 (306).

Shape shoulders

C.off 6 (7) sts beg next & foll alt rs 6 times in all. K 1 r.
C.off rem 6 (8) sts.
Work right front to match rev shaping.

SLEEVES

WY, c.on 120 (124) sts.
K few rs. Carr at right.
K 1 r in nylon cord.
Col B, RC 000, MT, K 14 rs.
MT + 3, K 1 r. MT, K 14 rs.
Turn up hem.
Col A, RC 000, MT, inc 1 st both ends next & ev foll 4th rs until 138 (142) sts.
Cont to K until RC 56.

Shape top

RC 000, c.off 5 (6) sts beg next 2 rs.
C.off 3 (4) sts beg next 2 rs.
C.off 2 sts beg next 24 (16) rs.
Dec 1 st both ends next & foll alt rs 24 (32) times in all.
26 sts rem. RC 76 (84).
C.off rem sts.

FRONT BANDS

(K two)
Bring forward 190 (196) ns.
With purl side facing pick up sts along one front to shoulder.
Col B, RC 000, MT, K 14 rs.
MT + 3, K 1 r. MT, K 14 rs.
C.off.

TO MAKE UP

Press all pieces.
Join shoulder seams.
Join & fold all bands to inside & slip st into pos.
Insert sleeves.
Sew side & sleeve seams.
Give final press.

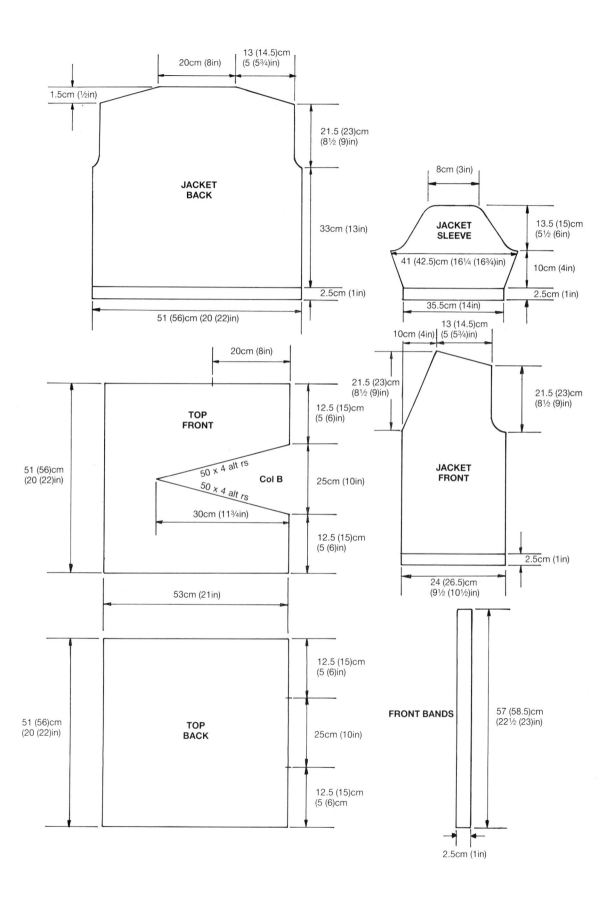

20cm (8in)

13 (14.5)cm
(5 (5¾)in)

1.5cm (½in)

21.5 (23)cm
(8½ (9)in)

**JACKET
BACK**

33cm (13in)

2.5cm (1in)

51 (56)cm (20 (22)in)

8cm (3in)

**JACKET
SLEEVE**

13.5 (15)cm
(5½ (6)in)

41 (42.5)cm (16¼ (16¾)in)

10cm (4in)

2.5cm (1in)

35.5cm (14in)

20cm (8in)

**TOP
FRONT**

12.5 (15)cm
(5 (6)in)

50 x 4 alt rs

Col B

50 x 4 alt rs

25cm (10in)

30cm (11¾in)

12.5 (15)cm
(5 (6)in)

51 (56)cm
(20 (22)in)

53cm (21in)

13 (14.5)cm
(5 (5¾)in)

10cm (4in)

21.5 (23)cm
(8½ (9)in)

21.5 (23)cm
(8½ (9)in)

**JACKET
FRONT**

2.5cm (1in)

24 (26.5)cm
(9½ (10½)in)

12.5 (15)cm
(5 (6)in)

**TOP
BACK**

25cm (10in)

51 (56)cm
(20 (22)in)

12.5 (15)cm
(5 (6)cm

FRONT BANDS

57 (58.5)cm
(22½ (23)in)

2.5cm (1in)

RC 000, T1/1, K 30 rs.
Trans sts to M/bed.
With K side facing, pick up sts evenly around sleeve edge.
T10, K 1 r.
C.off with latch tool.

WELTS
(K two)
Using standard gauge mach, col B, c.on in 1 × 1 rib 131 (135, 139) sts.
RC 000, T1/1, K 40 rs.

Trans sts to M/bed.
With K side facing pick up sts evenly along front or back waist.
T10, K 1 r.
C.off with latch tool.

TO MAKE UP
Join upper sleeve & shoulder seams.
Sew inside sleeve & side seams.
Roll neck to outside.
Press with warm iron.

(See photograph on page 96)

Sizes 81/86 (91/96, 102/107)cm (32/34 (36/38, 40/42)in)

Materials 1 cone BK Cotton Floss col A
1 cone BK 4-ply col B

Tension 16 sts × 32 rs = 10cm (4in)
T at approx 2

Notes Purl side is right side of garment.
The main body of the garment is knitted on a chunky mach & the welts on a standard gauge mach.

BACK & FRONT ALIKE
(K two)
To the right of cent 0, c.on in WY 30 sts.
K few rs, ending with carr at left.
K 1 r in nylon cord.
Col A, RC 000, MT, K 97 (101, 105) rs.
Carr at left, c.on 40 sts beg next r.
K 94 (98, 102) rs.
Mark right edge for cent.
K 95 (99, 103) rs.
Carr at left, c.off 40 sts beg next r.
K 96 (100, 104) rs.
RC 382 (398, 414).
K 1 r in nylon cord.
Rel work on WY.

NECKBANDS
(K two)
Bring forword 50 ns.
With K side facing pick up 25 sts each side of cent marker.
Col A, RC 000, MT, K 19 rs.
T10, K 1 r.
C.off with latch tool.

CUFFS
(K two)
Using standard gauge mach, col B, c.on in 1 × 1 rib 59 (63, 67) sts.

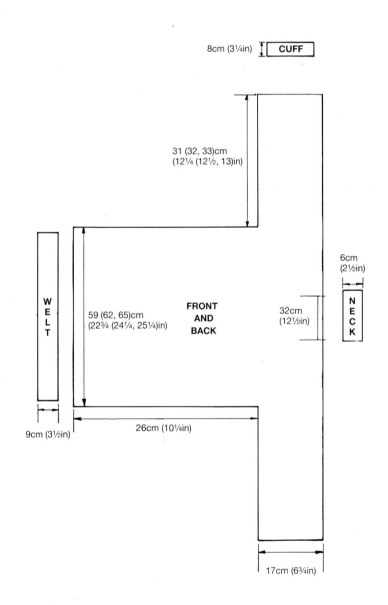

8cm (3¼in) | CUFF

31 (32, 33)cm (12¼ (12½, 13)in)

6cm (2½in)

W E L T

59 (62, 65)cm (22¾ (24¼, 25¼)in)

FRONT AND BACK

32cm (12½in)

N E C K

9cm (3½in)

26cm (10¼in)

17cm (6¾in)

Chunky 'V' frill neck sweater.

(See photograph on page 97)

Sizes 81/86 (91/97, 102/107)cm
(32/34 (36/38, 40/42)in)

Materials 1 cone BK Cotton Floss
col A
1 cone BK 4-ply col B

Tension 16 sts × 32 rs = 10cm
(4in)
T at approx 2

Notes Purl side is right side of
garment.
The main body of the garment is
knitted on a chunky mach & the
welts on a standard gauge mach.

BACK & FRONT ALIKE
(K two)
To the right of cent 0, c.on in
WY, 35 sts.
K few rs, ending with carr at left.
K 1 r in nylon cord.
Col A, RC 000, MT, K 96 (100,
104) rs.
Inc 1 st at left next & foll alt rs, 5
times in all, carr at left.
C.on 40 sts beg next r.
K 112 (115, 118) rs.
Mark right edge for cent.
K 111 (114, 117) rs, carr at left.
C.off 40 sts beg next r.
Dec 1 st at left next & foll alt rs.
5 times in all.
35 sts rem.
K 97 (101, 105) rs.
RC 436 (450, 464).
K 1 r in nylon cord.
Rel work on WY.

BACK NECK
Bring forward 50 ns.
With K side facing pick up 25 sts
each side of cent marker.
Col A, RC 000, MT, K 19 rs.
T10, K 1 r.
C.off with latch tool.

FRONT NECK
Bring forward 50 ns.
With K side facing, pick up 25 sts
each side of cent marker.
Col A, RC 000, MT, K 20 rs.
Dec 1 st both ends next & foll 4th
rs until 20 sts rem.
RC 78.
Dec 1 st both ends next & foll alt
rs until all sts have been dec.
C.off last st.

CUFFS
(K two)
Using standard gauge mach, col
B, c.on in 1 × 1 rib 61 (65, 69)
sts.
RC 000, T1/1, K 44 rs.
Trans sts to M/bed.
With K side facing pick up sts
evenly around sleeve edge.
T10, K 1 r.

C.off with latch tool.

WELTS
(K two)
Using standard gauge mach, col
B, c.on in 1 × 1 rib 131 (135,
139) sts.
RC 000, T1/1, K 44 rs.
Trans sts to M/bed.
With K side facing pick up sts
from front or back waist.
T10, K 1 r.
C.off with latch tool.

TO MAKE UP
Join upper sleeve & shoulder
seams.
Sew inside sleeve & side seams.
Col B, work 2 rs double crochet
around front neck.
Fold bands to outside.
Press with warm iron.

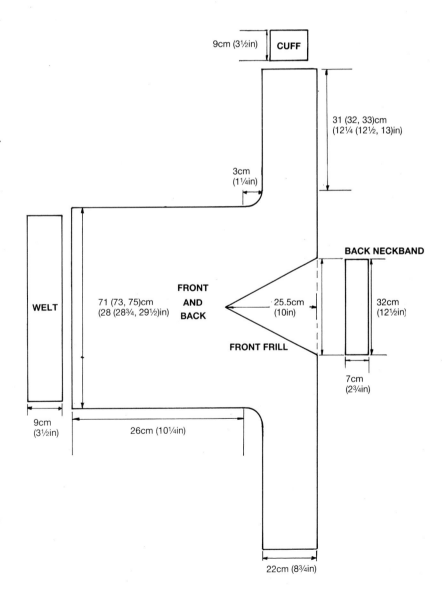

9cm (3½in) CUFF

31 (32, 33)cm
(12¼ (12½, 13)in)

3cm
(1¼in)

BACK NECKBAND

WELT

71 (73, 75)cm
(28 (28¾, 29½)in)

FRONT
AND
BACK

25.5cm
(10in)

32cm
(12½in)

FRONT FRILL

7cm
(2¾in)

9cm
(3½in)

26cm (10¼in)

22cm (8¾in)

Chunky Cocktail Fizz sweater.

(See photograph on page 100)

Sizes 81 (86, 91, 97, 102)cm (32 (34, 36, 38, 40)in)

Materials 15 (16, 16, 17, 18) 25g balls Argyll Cocktail Fizz, col A 1 ball Argyll Cocktail Fizz, col B

Tension 14 sts × 22 rs = 10cm (4in)
T at approx 6

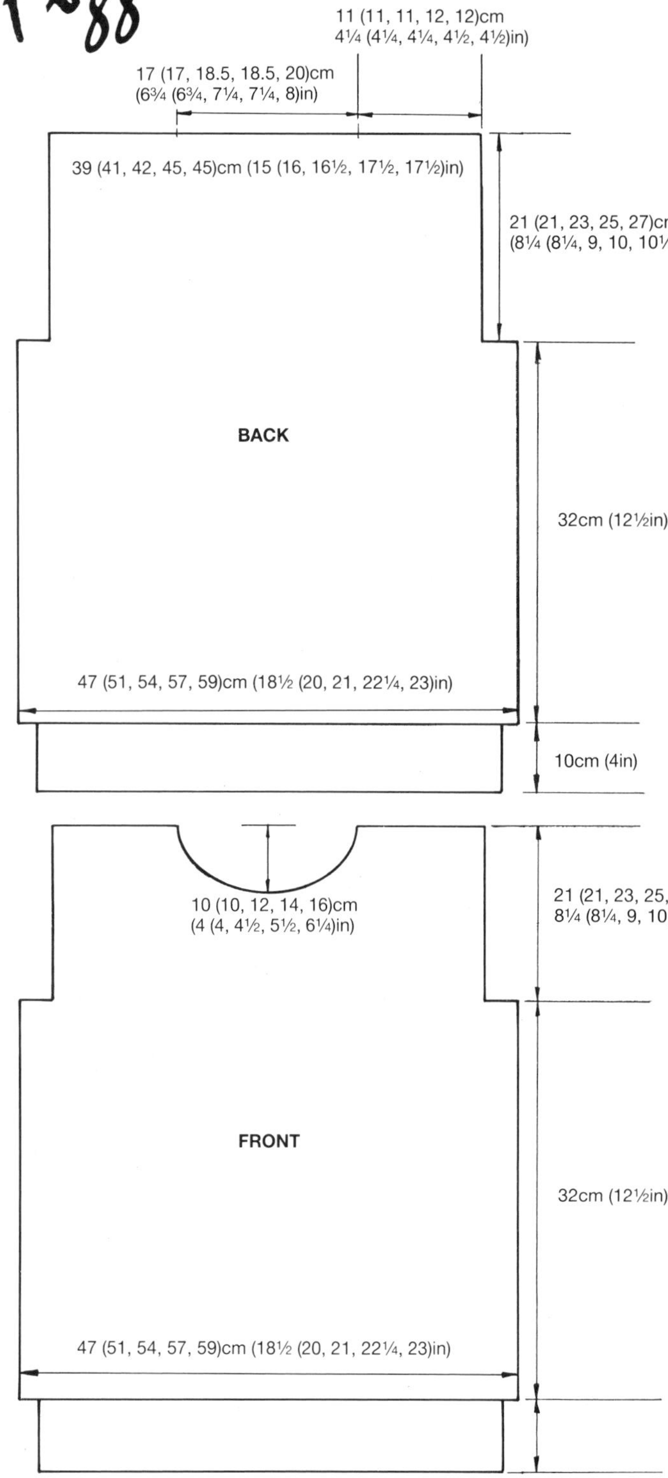

BACK

Col A, c.on in 1 × 1 rib 65 (69, 72, 79, 81) sts.
RC 000, T0/0, K 24 rs.
Trans sts to M/bed, inc 1 st.
RC 000, MT, K 70 rs.

Shape Armholes

C.off 6 (7, 8, 9, 10) sts beg next 2 rs*.
Cont to K until RC 116 (116, 120, 124, 128) rs.

Shape Shoulders

C.off 5 sts beg next 4 rs.
C.off 5 (6, 6, 7, 7) sts beg next 2 rs.
Rel rem 24 (24, 26, 26, 28) sts on WY.

FRONT

K as for back to *.
Cont to K until RC 94 (94, 110, 114, 118) rs.

Shape Neck

Divide work, place 30 (31, 33, 34, 36) sts at left into HP or K back on nylon cord.
Work on right side.
Always taking yarn round last n in HP, K 2 rs.
At neck edge push 3 sts into HP. K 2 rs.

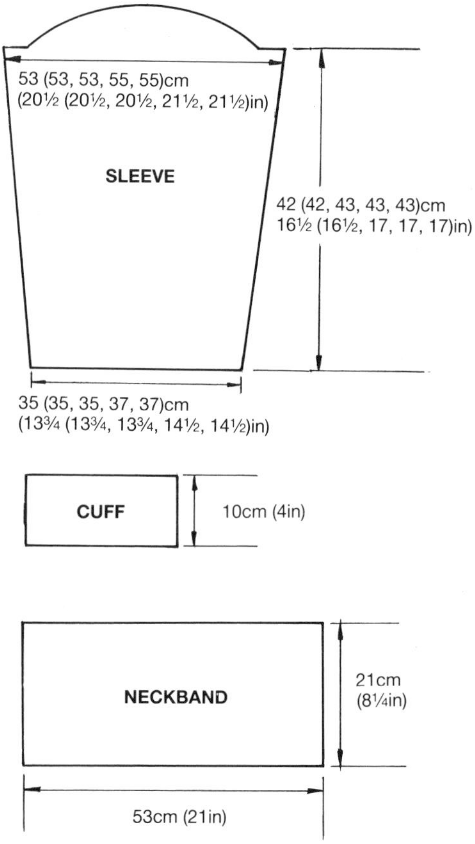

11 (11, 11, 12, 12)cm
4¼ (4¼, 4¼, 4½, 4½)in

17 (17, 18.5, 18.5, 20)cm
(6¾ (6¾, 7¼, 7¼, 8)in)

39 (41, 42, 45, 45)cm (15 (16, 16½, 17½, 17½)in)

21 (21, 23, 25, 27)cm
(8¼ (8¼, 9, 10, 10½)in)

BACK

32cm (12½in)

47 (51, 54, 57, 59)cm (18½ (20, 21, 22¼, 23)in)

10cm (4in)

10 (10, 12, 14, 16)cm
(4 (4, 4½, 5½, 6¼)in)

21 (21, 23, 25, 27)cm
8¼ (8¼, 9, 10, 10½)in

FRONT

32cm (12½in)

47 (51, 54, 57, 59)cm (18½ (20, 21, 22¼, 23)in)

53 (53, 53, 55, 55)cm
(20½ (20½, 20½, 21½, 21½)in)

SLEEVE

42 (42, 43, 43, 43)cm
16½ (16½, 17, 17, 17)in

35 (35, 35, 37, 37)cm
(13¾ (13¾, 13¾, 14½, 14½)in)

CUFF

10cm (4in)

NECKBAND

21cm (8¼in)

53cm (21in)

Push 2 sts into HP. K 2 rs.
Push 1 st into HP next & foll alt rs
until 15 (16, 16, 17, 17) sts rem.
Cont to K until RC 116 (116, 120,
124, 128) rs.

Shape Shoulder
C.off 5 sts beg next & foll alt r.
K 1 r.
C.off 4 (5, 5, 6, 6) sts beg next r.
Move the last st onto the 5th (5th,
7th, 9th, 11th) empty needle to
the right.
Pick up 4 (4, 6, 8, 10) sts at right
and leave in HP.
Break yarn.
Return 24 (25, 25, 26, 26) ns at
left to WP.
Work neck to match rev all
shaping.
DO NOT BREAK YARN.
MT, K 1 r across all ns.
Rel work on WY.

SLEEVES
Col A, c.on by hand 50 (50, 50,
52, 52) sts.

RC 000, MT, K 6 rs.
Inc 1 st both ends next & foll 6th
rs until 74 (74, 74, 76, 76) sts.
Cont to K until RC 92 (92, 94, 94,
94) rs.

Shape Top
C.off 6 (8, 9, 11, 12) sts beg next
2 rs.
Dec 1 st both ends next & foll alt
rs 0 (2, 3, 6, 8) times in all.
Dec 1 st both ends next & ev foll r
until 8 sts rem.
C.off.

CUFFS
(K two)
Col A, c.on in 1 × 1 rib 31 (31,
31, 35, 35) sts.
RC 000, T0/0, K 1 r.
Col B, K 2 rs. Col A, K 2 rs.
Col B, K 2 rs. Col A, K 4 rs.
Col B K 2 rs. Col A, K until RC
24 rs.
Trans sts to M/bed.
With wrong side facing pick up

sts evenly around sleeve edge.
MT + 1, K 1 r. T10, K 1 r.
C.off with latch tool.

NECKBAND
Col A, c.on in 1 × 1 rib 59 (59,
67, 71, 79) sts.
T1/1, work selvedge edge.
RC 000, T2/2, K 1 r.
Col B, K 2 rs. Col A, K 2 rs.
Col B, K 2 rs. Col A, K 4 rs.
Col B, K 2 rs. Col A, K 6 rs.
Col B, K 2 rs. Col A, K 3 rs.
T1/1, K 10 rs. T0/0, K 14 rs.
Trans sts to M/bed.
With wrong side facing pick up
sts held on WY at neck.
MT + 1, K 1 r. T10, K 1 r.
C.off very loosely.

TO MAKE UP
Join shoulder seams.
Insert sleeves.
Sew side and sleeve seams.
Join neckband and fold to front.
Brush with teasle brush.

Chunky roll neck sweater—see pattern on page 92

Chunky 'V' frill neck sweater—see pattern on page 93

Chunky polo neck sweater.

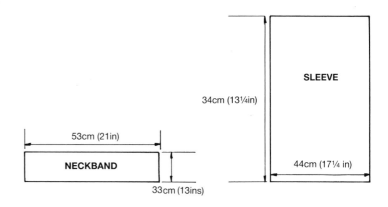

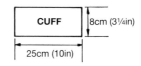

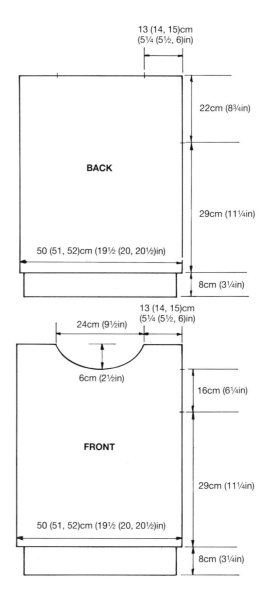

(See photograph on page 101)

Sizes 81/86 (91/97, 102/107)cm
(32/34 (36/38, 40/42)in)

Materials 1 cone BK Cotton Floss
col A
1 cone BK Charisma col B, used
two ends throughout

Tension 16 sts × 36 rs = 10cm
(4in)
T at approx 2

Note Purl side is used as right side
of garment

BACK
Col B, c.on in 1 × 1 rib 79 (81,
83) sts.
RC 000, T1/1, K 30 rs.
Trans sts to M/bed.
Change to col A, MT, K 100 rs.
Mark both edges.
Cont to K until RC 180.
C.off 21 (22, 23) sts beg next 2 rs.
Rel rem sts on WY.

FRONT
Col B, c.on in 1 × 1 rib 79 (81,
83) sts.
RC 000, T1/1, K 30 rs.
Trans sts to M/bed.
Change to col A, MT, K 100 rs.
Mark both edges.
Cont to K until RC 156.

Shape Neck
Push 52 ns at left into HP or K
back onto nylon cord.
Always taking yarn round last n in
HP, push 2 sts at left into HP next
& foll alt rs 4 times in all.
Dec 1 st beg next r.
Cont to K until RC 180.
C.off loosely.
Leave cent 19 sts in HP.
Work right side to match.
Rel cent sts on WY.

SLEEVES

WY, c.on 70 sts.
K few rs ending with carr at left.
K 1 r in nylon cord.
RC 000, col A, MT, K 120 rs.
C.off loosely

CUFFS

(K two)
Col B, c.on in 1 × 1 rib 39 sts.

RC 000, T1/1, K 30 rs.
Trans sts to M/bed.
With K side facing pick up sts
evenly from sleeve.
T2, K 1 r. T6, K 1 r.
C.off with latch tool.

NECKBAND

Col B, c.on in 1 × 1 rib 89 sts.
RC 000, T3/3, K 20 rs.
T2/2, K 20 rs. T1/1, K 20 rs. T0/0,
K 30 rs.

Trans sts to M/bed.
With wrong side facing pick up
sts around neck.
T7, K 1 r. T10, K 1 r.
C.off with latch tool.

TO MAKE UP

Join shoulder seams.
Sew sleeves between markers.
Join side and sleeve seams.
Join neckband.
Press with warm iron.

Chunky cocktail fizz sweater—see pattern on page 94

Chunky polo neck sweater—see pattern on page 98

Chunky short sleeved top

(See photograph on page 104)

Sizes 81 (86, 91, 97)cm (32 (34, 36, 38)in)

Materials 6 (7, 8, 8) balls Argyll Mistral

Tension 19 sts × 24 rs = 10cm (4in)
T at approx 2

Note Purl side is right side of garment

BACK
WY, c.on 86 (90, 96, 100) sts.
K few rs. Carr at left.
K 1 r in nylon cord*.
MY, RC 000, MT, K 114 (118, 120, 124) rs.

Shape shoulders
C.off 13 (15, 18, 20) sts beg next 2 rs.
Rel rem 60 (60, 62, 62) sts on WY.

FRONT
K as for back to *.
MY, RC 000, MT, K 96 (100, 102, 106) rs.

Shape neck
Place 63 (65, 68, 70) sts at left into HP or K back onto nylon cord.
Work on right side only.
Always taking yarn round last n in HP, push 1 st into HP next 10 rs.
Cont to K until RC 114 (118, 129, 124).

Shape shoulder
C.off rem 13 (15, 18, 20) sts.
Return 23 (25, 28, 30) sts at left to WP.
K as for right side rev shaping.
Rel cent 60 sts on WY.

SLEEVES
C.on in 1 × 1 rib 59 (59, 69, 69) sts.
RC 000, T0/0, K 10 rs.
Trans sts to M/bed.
RC 000, MT, inc 1 st both ends next & foll 3rd rs, 11 times in all until 81 (81, 91, 91) sts rem.
Cont to K until RC 38.
C.off very loosely.

NECKBAND
Bring forward 128 ns.
With K side facing pick up sts held on WY at back, 4 sts down front shaping, 60 sts held on WY at front, 4 sts up front shaping.
RC 000, MT, K 6 rs. MT + 1, K 6 rs. MT + 2, K 2 rs.
C.off very loosely.

WELTS
(K two)
C.on in 1 × 1 rib 69 (71, 73, 75) sts.
RC 000, T0/0, K 24 rs.
Trans sts to M/bed.
With knit side facing pick up sts evenly along waist.
Mt + 1, K 1 r. T10, K 1 r.
C.off with latch tool.

To make up
Join shoulder seams.
Insert sleeves.
Sew side & sleeve seams.
Allow neckband to roll to front.
Press lightly.

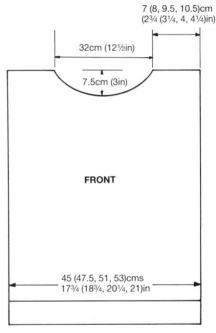

7 (8, 9.5, 10.5)cm (2¾ (3¼, 4, 4¼)in)

32cm (12½in)

7.5cm (3in)

FRONT

45 (47.5, 51, 53)cms
17¾ (18¾, 20¼, 21)in

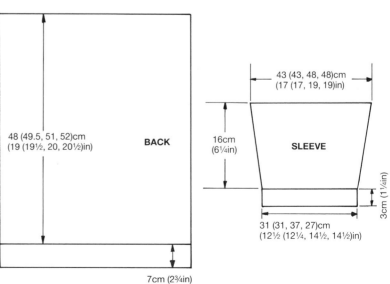

48 (49.5, 51, 52)cm (19 (19½, 20, 20½)in)

BACK

7cm (2¾in)

43 (43, 48, 48)cm (17 (17, 19, 19)in)

16cm (6¼in)

SLEEVE

3cm (1¼in)

31 (31, 37, 27)cm (12½ (12¼, 14½, 14½)in)

Join raglans leaving left back open.

FRONT NECKBAND
C.on in 1 × 1 rib 67 (71, 87, 95, 97) sts.
RC 000, T0/0, K 20 rs.
Trans sts to M/bed.
With wrong side facing pick up sts – 15 (21, 23, 25, 25) from left sleeve, 37 (39, 41, 45, 47) from front, 15 (21, 23, 25, 25) from

right sleeve.
MT, K 2 rs.
C.off with latch tool.

BACK NECKBAND
C.on in 1 × 1 rib 37 (39, 41, 45, 47) sts.
K as for front band pick up sts from back.

TO MAKE UP
Join side & sleeve seams.
Join band.

(See photograph on page 105)

Sizes 71 (76, 81, 86, 91)cm (28 (30, 32, 34, 36)in)

Materials 1 cone Bramwell Opal

Tension 11 sts × 18 rs = 10cm (4in)
T at approx 10

BACK & FRONT
(K two)
C.on in 1 × 1 rib 55 (59, 63, 67, 71) sts.
RC 000, T1/1, K 30 rs.
Rel work on WY.
Bring forward 48 (50, 52, 56, 58) ns on M/bed.
Rehang work, dec evenly across row.
RC 000, MT, K 56 rs.

Shape armholes
C.off 2 sts beg next 2 rs.
Dec 1 st both ends next & foll alt rs until 36 (38, 40, 44, 46) sts rem.
K 2 rs.
C.off rem sts.

SLEEVES
C.on in 1 × 1 rib 37 (41, 43, 43, 47) sts.
RC 000, T1/1, K 20 rs.
Rel work on WY.
Bring forward 28 (34, 36, 38, 38) ns on M/bed.
Rehang work, dec evenly along row.
RC 000, MT, K 36 (38, 38, 38, 38) rs.

Shape top
C.off 2 sts beg next 2 rs.
Dec. 1 st both ends next & foll alt rs until 16 (22, 24, 26, 26) sts rem.
K 2 rs.
C.off rem sts.

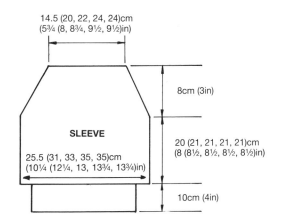

33 (35, 37, 40, 42)cm
(13 (13¾, 14½, 16, 16¾)in)

8cm (3in)

BACK & FRONT

31cm (12½in)

43 (45.5, 48, 50.5, 53)cm
(17 (18, 19, 20, 21)in)

12.5cm (5in)

14.5 (20, 22, 24, 24)cm
(5¾ (8, 8¾, 9½, 9½)in)

8cm (3in)

SLEEVE

20 (21, 21, 21, 21)cm
(8 (8½, 8½, 8½, 8½)in)

25.5 (31, 33, 35, 35)cm
(10¼ (12¼, 13, 13¾, 13¾)in)

10cm (4in)

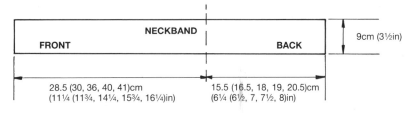

9cm (3½in)

| | **NECKBAND** | |
| **FRONT** | | **BACK** |

28.5 (30, 36, 40, 41)cm
(11¼ (11¾, 14¼, 15¾, 16¼)in)

15.5 (16.5, 18, 19, 20.5)cm
(6¼ (6½, 7, 7½, 8)in)

Chunky short sleeved top—see pattern on page 102

Chunky top —see pattern on page 103

Chunky Dolman sweater & Leg warmers.

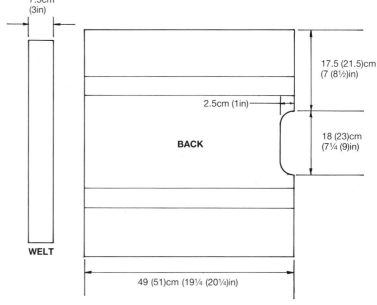

7.5cm (3in)

17.5 (21.5)cm (7 (8½)in)

2.5cm (1in)

BACK

18 (23)cm (7¼ (9)in)

WELT

49 (51)cm (19¼ (20¼)in)

CUFF 7.5cm (3in)

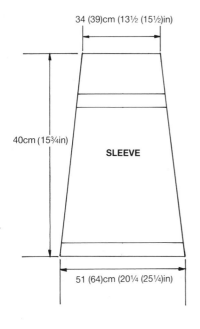

34 (39)cm (13½ (15½)in)

40cm (15¾in)

SLEEVE

51 (64)cm (20¼ (25¼)in)

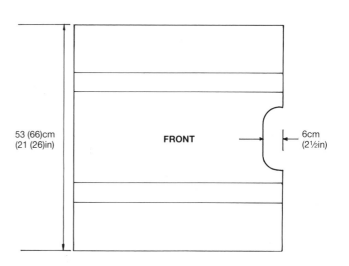

53 (66)cm (21 (26)in)

FRONT

6cm (2½in)

(See photograph on page 108)

Sizes 81/91 (97/107)cm (32/36 (38/42)in)

Materials 1 cone Bramwell Opal col A

1 cone Bramwell 4-ply col B used two ends throughout

Tension 16 sts × 24 rs = 10cm (4in)

T at approx 4

BACK

Col A, c.on by hand 77 (81) sts.
RC 000, MT, K 22 (32) rs.
Col B, K 10 rs. Col A, K 10 rs*.

Shape neck

Dec 1 st at right beg next 5 rs.
K 34 (44) rs.
Inc 1 st at right beg next 5 rs.
K 10 rs.
Col B, K 10 rs. Col A, K 22 (32) rs.
RC 128 (158).
C.off.

FRONT

K as for back to *.

Shape neck

Dec 1 st at right next 10 rs. K 24 (34) rs.
Inc 1 st at right next 10 rs. K 10 rs.
Col B, K 10 rs. Col A, K 22 (32) rs.
RC 128 (158).
C. off.

SLEEVES

Join shoulder seams.
Bring forward 82 (102) ns.
With purl side facing & shoulder seam at cent 0 pick up sts either side cent.

At same time

Col B, K 3 rs.
Dec 1 st both ends next & foll 4th rs until RC 10.
Col A, cont to dec ev 4th rs until 54 (62) sts rem on RC 76.
Col B, K 10 rs.
Cont in col A until RC 94.
Rel work on WY.

WELTS

(K two)
Col A, c.on in 1 × 1 rib 63 (67) sts.
RC 000, T1/1, K 20 rs.
Trans sts to M/bed.
With purl side facing pick up sts from back or front waist.
MT, K 1 r. T10, K 1 r.
C.off with latch tool.

CUFFS

(K two)
Col A, c.on in 1 × 1 rib 27 (31) sts.
RC 000, T1/1, K 20 rs.
Trans sts to M/bed.
With purl side facing pick up sts around sleeve edge placing 2 sts on each n.

MT, K 1 r. T10, K 1 r.
C.off with latch tool.

NECKBAND

Col A, c.on in 1 × 1 rib 75 (85) sts.
RC 000, T0/0, K 20 rs.
T1/1, K 10 rs. T2/2, K 9 rs.
T10/10, K 1 r.
Trans sts to M/bed.
C.off with latch tool working a chain st between each n.

TO MAKE UP

Join side & sleeve seams.
With c.on edge to garment, backstitch neckband to garment & fold to front.
Press very lightly.

Leg Warmers

Col A, c.on in 1 × 1 rib 49 (59) sts.
(K 5 rs circular).
RC 000, T1/1, K 139 rs.
Col B, K 10 rs.
Col A, K 9 rs. RC 158.
Trans sts to M/bed.
C.off loosely.

TO MAKE UP

Join side seam & fold top to front.
Press very lightly.

Chunky Dolman sweater & leg warmers—see pattern on page 106

Unisex Fisherman's rib sweater—see pattern on page 110

Unisex Fishermans rib sweater.

(See photograph on page 109)

Sizes 86 (91, 97, 102, 107, 112)cm (34 (36, 38, 40, 42, 44)in)

Materials 1 cone Bramwell fine 4-ply

Tensions 27 sts × 66 rs = 10cm (4in)
T at approx 4/4

BACK
C.on in 1 × 1 rib 125 (131, 139, 145, 153, 159) sts.
RC 000, T1/1, K 36 rs.

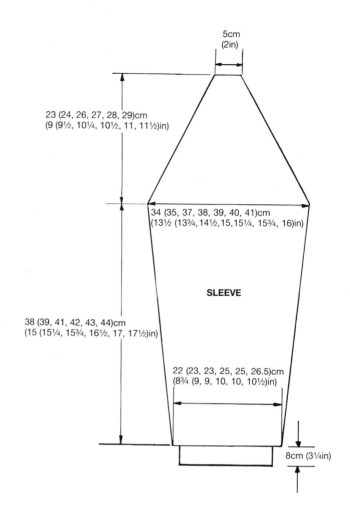

5cm (2in)

23 (24, 26, 27, 28, 29)cm (9 (9½, 10¼, 10½, 11, 11½)in)

34 (35, 37, 38, 39, 40, 41)cm (13½ (13¾, 14½, 15, 15¼, 15¾, 16)in)

SLEEVE

38 (39, 41, 42, 43, 44)cm (15 (15¼, 15¾, 16½, 17, 17½)in)

22 (23, 23, 25, 25, 26.5)cm (8¾ (9, 9, 10, 10, 10½)in)

8cm (3¼in)

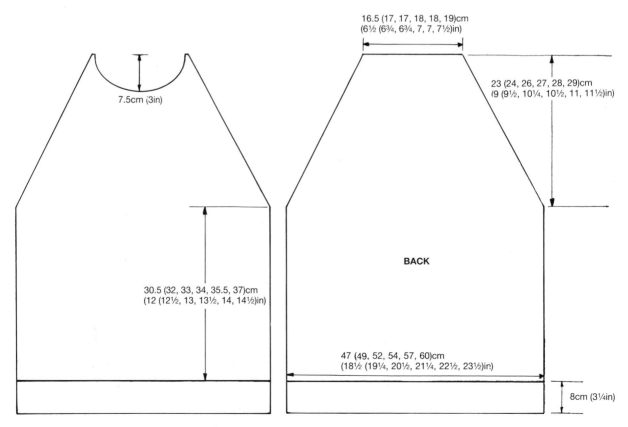

7.5cm (3in)

30.5 (32, 33, 34, 35.5, 37)cm (12 (12½, 13, 13½, 14, 14½)in)

16.5 (17, 17, 18, 18, 19)cm (6½ (6¾, 6¾, 7, 7, 7½)in)

23 (24, 26, 27, 28, 29)cm (9 (9½, 10¼, 10½, 11, 11½)in)

BACK

47 (49, 52, 54, 57, 60)cm (18½ (19¼, 20½, 21¼, 22½, 23½)in)

8cm (3¼in)

Set carr for Fisherman's rib.
RC 000, MT, K 198 (206, 214, 222, 232, 240) rs*.

Shape raglans

RC 000, dec 1 st both ends both beds next & foll 8th rs 19 (20, 17, 17, 15, 15) times in all. K 5 rs.
RC 150 (158, 134, 134, 118, 118).
49 (51, 71, 73, 93, 99) sts.
Dec 1 st both ends both beds next & foll 6th rs 1 (1, 6, 7, 11, 12) times in all.
45 (47, 47, 49, 49, 51) sts rem.
K 1 (1, 5, 5, 5, 5) rs. RC 152 (160, 170, 176, 184, 190).
Set carr 1 × 1 rib.
Rel work on WY.

FRONT

K as for back to *.

Shape raglans

RC 000, dec 1 st both ends both beds next & foll 8th rs 14 (15, 16, 16, 15, 15) times in all.
K 5 rs. RC 110 (118, 126, 126, 118, 118).
69 (71, 75, 81, 93, 99) sts.
Dec 1 st both ends both beds next & foll 6th rs 0 (0, 0, 0, 2, 3) times in all.
69 (71, 75, 81, 85, 87) sts rem.
RC 110 (118, 126, 126, 125, 131).

K 4 (4, 0, 4, 5, 5) rs.
RC 114 (122, 126, 130, 130, 136).
Divide work.
Push 41 (43, 45, 49, 51, 53) sts at left into HP.
Work on right side only.

Shape neck

Dec 1 st at neck edge next & foll alt rs.

At same time

dec 1 st both beds at raglan on 5th (5th, 7th, 7th, 7th, 1st, 1st) rs, then ev foll 8th (8th, 6th, 6th, 6th, 6th) rs until 8 (8, 8, 10, 10, 10) sts rem.
Cont to shape at raglan from last dec until 6 sts rem.
Dec 1 st at raglan next & foll 6th r. K 1 r.
C.off rem 2 sts.
Set carr 1 × 1 rib rel cent sts on WY.

SLEEVES

C.on in 1 × 1 rib 59 (63, 63, 67, 67, 71) sts.
RC 000, T1/1, K 36 rs.
Set carr for Fisherman's rib.
RC 000, MT, K 11 rs.
Inc 1 st both ends both beds next & foll 12th rs until 91 (95, 99,103, 107, 111) sts.
Cont to K until RC 248 (256, 264,

272, 280, 288).

Shape top

RC 000, dec 1 st both ends both beds next & foll 10th (10th, 10th, 10th, 10th, 8th) rs until 75 (79, 87, 97, 99, 95) sts.
Inc 1 st both ends both beds next & foll 8th rs until 15 sts rem.
K 1 (1, 5, 5, 7, 5) rs.
RC 152 (160, 170, 176, 186, 190).
Set carr 1 × 1 rib rel work on WY.

NECKBAND

Join three raglan seams leaving left back open.
C.on in 1 × 1 rib 135 (139, 141, 147, 149, 153) sts.
RC 000, T2/2, K 4 rs. T1/1, K 32 rs.
T2/2, K 3 rs. T3/3, K 1 r.
Trans sts to M/bed.
With wrong side facing pick up sts from sleeve, front sleeve & back neck.
MT + 2, K 1 r. T10, K 1 r.
C.off with latch tool.

TO MAKE UP

Join raglan.
Sew side & sleeve seams.
Fold neckband to inside & slip st into pos.
Press very lightly.

Unisex 'V' neck classic sweater.

Shape neck

Dec 1 st at neck next & foll 4th rs, 3 times in all. K 3 rs.
RC 132 (138, 144, 148, 154, 160, 166, 176).

Shape neck & armhole

At same time cont to dec 1 st at cent next & foll 4th rs.
Col A, RC 000, c.off 8 (8, 9, 10, 11, 12, 12, 13) sts beg next r.
K 1 r. Dec 1 st at arm next & foll alt rs 8 (10, 10, 11, 12, 13, 15, 16) times in all.

Cont to dec 1 st at cent ev foll 4th rs until 32 (33, 35, 36, 38, 39, 40, 40) sts rem.
Cont to K until RC 80 (84, 88, 92, 98, 100, 102, 104).

Shape shoulder

C.off 8 (8, 9, 9, 10, 10, 10, 11) sts beg next & foll alt rs, 3 times in all. K 1 r.
C.off rem 8 (9, 8, 9, 8, 9, 10, 7) sts.
Complete left side rev. shaping.

Sleeves

Col A, c.on in 1 × 1 rib 67 (69,

Sizes 81 (86, 91, 97, 102, 107, 112, 117)cm (32 (34, 36, 38, 40, 42, 44, 46)in)

Materials 1 cone Bramwell Ivette col A
1 cone Bramwell Ivette col B

Tension 32 sts × 44 rs = 10cm (4in)
T at approx 3

BACK

Col A, c.on in 1 × 1 rib 139 (147, 155, 163, 171, 179, 187, 191) sts.
RC 000, T0/0, K 30 rs.
Trans sts to M/bed. Inc 1 st.
RC 000, MT, K 58 (64, 70, 74, 80, 86, 92, 96) rs.
Col B, K 12 rs. Col A, K 24 rs*.
Col B, K 38 rs. RC 132 (138, 144, 148, 154, 160, 166, 170).

Shape armholes

Col A, RC 000.
C.off 8 (8, 9, 10, 11, 12, 12, 13) sts beg next 2 rs.
Dec 1 st both ends next & foll alt rs until 108 (112, 118, 122, 126, 130, 134, 134) sts rem.
Cont to K until RC 80 (84, 88, 92, 98, 100, 102, 104).

Shape shoulders

C.off 8 (8, 9, 9, 10, 10, 10, 11) sts beg next 6 rs.
C.off 8 (9, 8, 9, 8, 9, 10, 7) sts beg next 2 rs.
Rel cent 44 (46, 48, 50, 50, 52, 54, 54) sts on WY.

FRONT

K as for back to *.
Col B, K 26 rs. RC 120 (126, 132, 136, 142, 148, 154, 158).

Divide work

Push all ns left cent 0 into HP or K

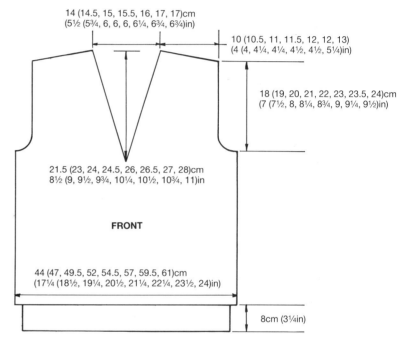

14 (14.5, 15, 15.5, 16, 17, 17)cm
(5½ (5¾, 6, 6, 6, 6¼, 6¾, 6¾)in)

10 (10.5, 11, 11.5, 12, 12, 13)
(4 (4, 4¼, 4¼, 4½, 4½, 5¼)in)

18 (19, 20, 21, 22, 23, 23.5, 24)cm
(7 (7½, 8, 8¼, 8¾, 9, 9¼, 9½)in)

21.5 (23, 24, 24.5, 26, 26.5, 27, 28)cm
8½ (9, 9½, 9¾, 10¼, 10½, 10¾, 11)in

FRONT

44 (47, 49.5, 52, 54.5, 57, 59.5, 61)cm
(17¼ (18½, 19¼, 20½, 21¼, 22¼, 23½, 24)in)

8cm (3¼in)

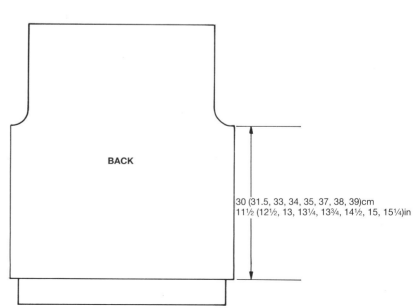

BACK

30 (31.5, 33, 34, 35, 37, 38, 39)cm
11½ (12½, 13, 13¼, 13¾, 14½, 15, 15¼)in

71, 73, 77, 83, 87, 91) sts.
RC 000, T0/0, K 30 rs.
Trans sts to M/bed.
RC 000, MT, K 2 rs.
Inc 1 st both ends next & foll 8th
rs until RC 80 (90, 102, 112, 112,
112, 112, 124).
Cont to inc as before and work
stripes.
Col B, K 12 rs. Col A, K 24 rs.
Col B, cont to inc as before until
103 (107, 111, 117, 125, 131,
135, 139) sts.
Cont in col B until RC 154 (164,
176, 186, 186, 186, 186, 198).

Shape armholes

Col A, RC 000, c.off 7 (7, 7, 8, 9,
10, 11, 12) sts beg next 2 rs.
Dec 1 st both ends next & foll alt
rs until RC 10.
Dec 1 st both ends next & foll 4th
rs until RC 18 (18, 18, 18, 18, 18,
22, 22).
Dec 1 st both ends next & foll alt
rs until RC 52 (56, 58, 62, 66, 66,
68, 68).
Dec 1 st both ends next 10 rs.
C.off rem sts.

NECKBAND

1st side
Join right shoulder seam.
Col A, c.on in 1 × 1 rib 111 (113,
119, 125, 129, 135, 141, 145)
sts.
RC 000, T0/0, K 1 r.
Inc 1 st at left next & foll alt rs.
At same time
T0/0, K 6 rs. T1/1, K 6 rs.
T2/2, K 3 rs. T3/3, K 1 r.
Trans sts to M/bed.
With wrong side facing pick up
sts from cent V and across back
placing shaped edge at cent.
MT + 2, K 1 r. T10, K 1 r.
C.off with latch tool.

2nd side
Col A, c.on in 1 × 1 rib 63 (67,
71, 75, 79, 83, 87, 91) sts.
K as above picking up sts from
cent V to shoulder.

TO MAKE UP
Join shoulder seam.
Insert sleeves.
Sew side & sleeve seams.
Join cent V.
Press with cool iron.

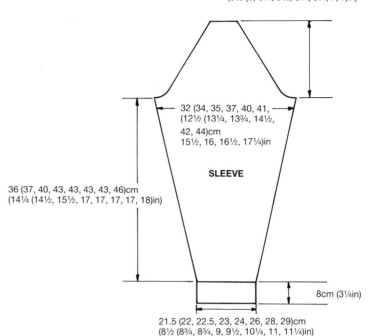

14 (15, 16, 16.5, 17, 17, 18, 18)cm
(5½, 6, 6¼, 6½, 6¾, 6¾, 7, 7)in)

32 (34, 35, 37, 40, 41,
(12½ (13¼, 13¾, 14½,
42, 44)cm
15½, 16, 16½, 17¼)in)

SLEEVE

36 (37, 40, 43, 43, 43, 43, 46)cm
(14¼ (14½, 15½, 17, 17, 17, 17, 18)in)

8cm (3¼in)

21.5 (22, 22.5, 23, 24, 26, 28, 29)cm
(8½ (8¾, 8¾, 9, 9½, 10¼, 11, 11¼)in)

Unisex Intarsia sweater.

(See photograph on page 116)

Sizes 86 (91, 97, 102, 107, 112)cm (34(36, 38, 40, 42, 44)in)

Materials: 1 cone each BK 4-ply Acrylic in 5 shades
Intarsia chart (page 119)

Tension: 28 sts × 40 rs = 10cm (4in) at approx 6

BACK
Col A, c.on in 1 × 1 rib 125 (133, 139, 147, 153, 159) sts.
RC 000, T1/1, K 40 rs.
Trans sts to M/bed. Inc 1 st.
RC 000, MT, K 140 (140, 140, 160, 160, 160) rs.

Shape armholes
C.off 10 sts beg next 2 rs.
Cont to K until RC 230 (234, 238, 262, 266, 270).

Shape shoulders
C.off 7 (9, 10, 11, 12, 13) sts beg next 2 rs.
C.off 8 (9, 10, 11, 12, 13) sts beg next 2 rs.
C.off 8 (9, 10, 12, 13, 14) sts beg next 2 rs.
Rel rem 60 sts on WY.

FRONT
K as for back working from Intarsia chart to RC 190 (194, 198, 222, 226, 230).

Shape neck
Push 63 (67, 70, 74, 77, 80) ns at left into HP or K back on nylon cord.
Work on right side only, always taking yarn round last n in HP.
At neck edge push 3 sts into HP next & foll alt rs 3 times in all.
Push 2 sts into HP next & foll alt rs 3 times in all.
Push 1 st into HP next & foll alt rs 5 times in all.
23 (27, 30, 34, 37, 40) sts rem in WP.
Cont to K until RC 230 (234, 238, 262, 266, 270).

Shape shoulder
C.off 7 (9, 10, 11, 12, 13) sts beg next r. K 1 r.
C.off 8 (9, 10, 11, 12, 13) sts beg next r. K 1 r.
C.off 8 (9, 10, 12, 13, 14) sts beg next r.
Bring 43 (47, 50, 54, 57, 60) sts at left back into WP.
Work left side to match rev shaping.
Pick up 11 sts each side cent.
K 1 r across all ns.
Rel work on WY.

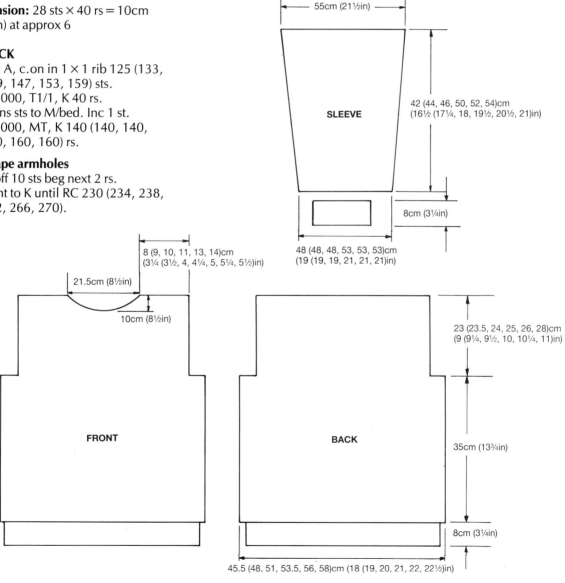

SLEEVE

55cm (21½in)

42 (44, 46, 50, 52, 54)cm (16½ (17¼, 18, 19½, 20½, 21)in)

8cm (3¼in)

48 (48, 48, 53, 53, 53)cm (19 (19, 19, 21, 21, 21)in)

FRONT

8 (9, 10, 11, 13, 14)cm (3¼ (3½, 4, 4¼, 5, 5½)in)

21.5cm (8½in)

10cm (8½in)

BACK

23 (23.5, 24, 25, 26, 28)cm (9 (9¼, 9½, 10, 10¼, 11)in)

35cm (13¾in)

8cm (3¼in)

45.5 (48, 51, 53.5, 56, 58)cm (18 (19, 20, 21, 22, 22½)in)

Unisex Intarsia sweater—see pattern on page 115

Motor bike sweater—see pattern on page 126

1st SLEEVE

*WY, c.on 118 (122, 126, 138, 146, 150) sts.
K few rs. Carr at left.
K 1 r in nylon cord.
RC 000, MT, K 5 rs.
Inc 1 st both ends next & ev foll 6th rs until 130 (134, 138, 150, 158, 162) sts.
Cont to K until RC 100 (100, 100, 120, 120, 120)*.
Col C, K 20 rs. Col B, K 20 rs.
Col A, cont to K until RC 190 (190, 190, 210, 210, 210).
C.off loosely.

2nd SLEEVE

K as for first sleeve from * to *.
Cont to K until RC 100 (100, 100, 120, 120, 120).
Col D, K 20 rs. Col E, K 20 rs.
Col A, cont to K until RC 190 (190, 190, 210, 210, 210).
C.off loosely.

CUFFS

(K two)
Col A, c.on in 1 × 1 rib 59 (61, 63, 69, 73, 77) sts.
RC 000, T1/1, K 40 rs.
Trans sts to M/bed.
With wrong side facing pick up sts around sleeve.
T7, K 1 r. T10, K 1 r.
C.off with latch tool.

NECKBAND

Col A, c.on in 1 × 1 rib 143 sts.
RC 000, T4/4, K 2 rs.
T3/3, K 2 rs. T2/2, K 12 rs.
T5/5, K 1 r. T2/2, K 12 rs.
T3/3, K 2 rs. T4/4, K 2 rs.
Trans sts to M/bed.
With wrong side facing pick up sts from neck – 60 back, 11 side front shaping, 60 across cent, 11 up front shaping.
T7, K 1 r. T10, K 1 r.
C.off with latch tool.

TO MAKE UP

Join shoulder seams.
Insert sleeves.
Sew side & sleeve seams.
Fold neckband to inside & slip st into position.
Press with cool iron.

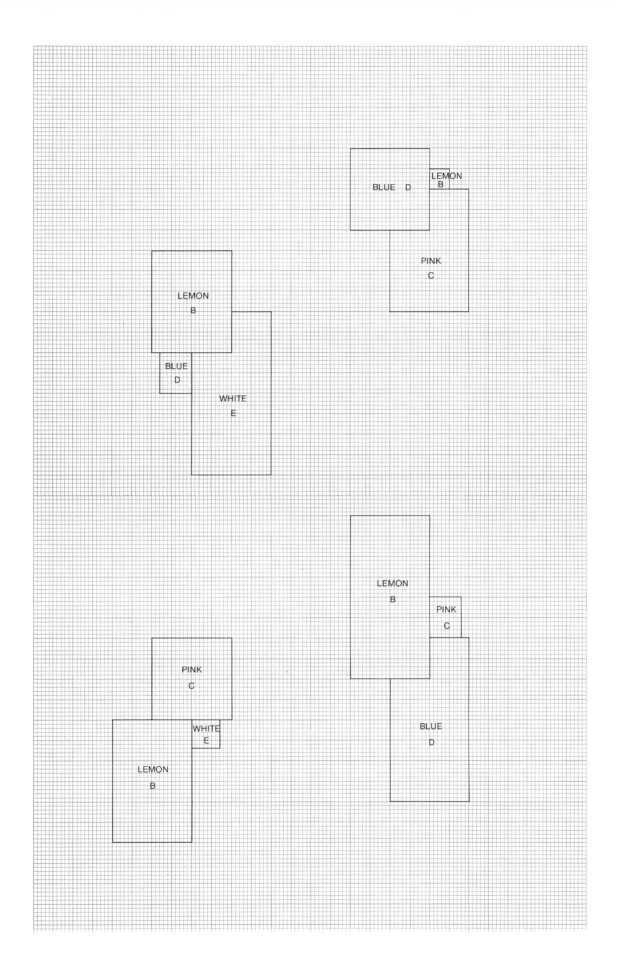

Summer top

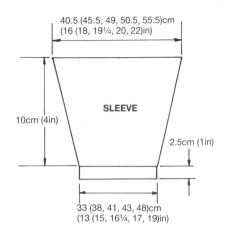

40.5 (45.5, 49, 50.5, 55.5)cm
(16 (18, 19¼, 20, 22)in)

SLEEVE

10cm (4in)

2.5cm (1in)

33 (38, 41, 43, 48)cm
(13 (15, 16¼, 17, 19)in)

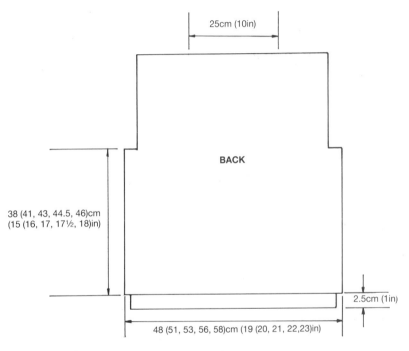

25cm (10in)

BACK

38 (41, 43, 44.5, 46)cm
(15 (16, 17, 17½, 18)in)

2.5cm (1in)

48 (51, 53, 56, 58)cm (19 (20, 21, 22,23)in)

Sizes 91 (97, 102, 107, 112)cm
(36 (38, 40, 42, 44)in)

Materials 1 cone Bramwell
Tweedknit col A
1 cone Bramwell fine 4-ply col B
3 buttons

Tension 28 sts × 40 rs = 10cm
(4in)
T at approx 7

BACK
Col A, c.on in 1 × 1 rib 133 (139,
147, 153, 161) sts.
RC 000, T1/1, K 20 rs.
Trans sts to M/bed. Inc 1 st.
RC 000, K 150 (160, 170, 176,
180) rs.

Shape armholes
C.off 10 sts beg next 2 rs*.
Cont to K until RC 230 (250, 266,
276, 290).

Shape shoulder
C.off 7 (8, 9, 10, 12) sts beg next
4 rs.
C.off 8 (9, 11, 12, 12) sts beg next
2 rs.
Rel rem 70 sts on WY.

FRONT
K as for back to *.
Cont to K until RC 170 (190, 206,
216, 230).
Divide work.
C.off cent 6 sts.
Push all sts at left into HP or K
back onto nylon cord.
Cont to K until RC 210 (230, 246,
256, 270).

Shape neck
Always taking yarn round last ns
in HP at oppos end to carr push
11 sts into HP end next r. K 1 r.
Push 3 sts into HP next & foll alt rs

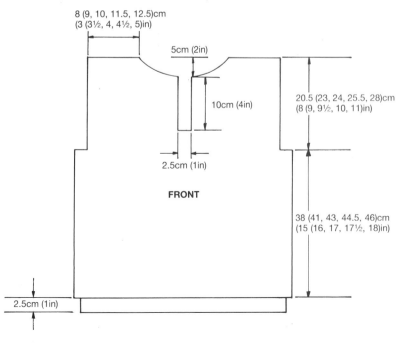

8 (9, 10, 11.5, 12.5)cm
(3 (3½, 4, 4½, 5)in)

5cm (2in)

10cm (4in)

2.5cm (1in)

20.5 (23, 24, 25.5, 28)cm
(8 (9, 9½, 10, 11)in)

FRONT

38 (41, 43, 44.5, 46)cm
(15 (16, 17, 17½, 18)in)

2.5cm (1in)

7 times in all.
22 (25, 29, 32, 36) sts rem.
Cont to K until RC 230 (250, 266, 276, 290).

Shape shoulder

C.off 7 (8, 9, 10, 11) sts beg next & foll alt r. K 1 r.
C.off rem 8 (9, 11, 12, 12) sts.
Work left side to match rev shaping.

SLEEVES

Col A, c.on in 1 × 1 rib 91 (105, 113, 119, 133) sts.
RC 000, T2/2, K 10 rs.
Trans sts to M/bed. Inc 1 st.
RC 000, MT, K 2 rs.
Inc 1 st both ends next & foll 4th rs 10 times in all.

112 (126, 134, 140, 154) sts.
Cont to K until RC 44.
Col B, K 2 rs.
K 16 rs.
C.off loosely.

NECKBAND

(K two)
Col B, c.on in 1 × 1 rib 73 sts.
RC 000, T1/1, K 8 rs. T2/2, K 1 r.
T4/4, K 1 r.
Trans sts to M/bed.
With purl side facing pick up sts around front neck to cent back.
MT, K 1 r. T10, K 1 r.
C.off with latch tool.

FRONT BAND

Col B, c.on in 1 × 1 rib 43 sts.
RC 000, T2/2, K 9 rs. T4/4, K 1 r.
Trans sts to M/bed.

With purl side facing pick up sts on right front from cent to top of neck band.
RC 000, MT, K 1 r. T10, K 1 r.
C.off with latch tool.

BUTTON BAND

K as above working 3 small buttonholes over 5th r.

TO MAKE UP

Press all pieces.
Join shoulder seams.
Insert sleeves placing col B to c.off sts.
Sew side and sleeve seams.
Sew bands to cent front & join back.
Sew on 3 buttons.
Press.

Cardigan.

(See photograph on page 125)

Sizes 91 (97, 102, 107, 112)cm
(36 (38, 40, 42, 44)in)

Materials 2 cones BK Superwash
wool
7 buttons

Tension 28 sts × 40 rs = 10cm
(4in)
T at approx 6

BACK
C.on in 2 × 2 rib 132 (140, 148,
156, 164) sts.
RC 000, T2/2, K 30 rs.
Trans sts to M/bed.
RC 000, MT, K 154 rs.

Shape armholes
C.off 10 sts beg next 2 rs.
Cont to K until RC 244.

Shape shoulder
C.off 21 (25, 29, 33, 37) sts beg
next 2 rs.
C.off rem sts.

RIGHT FRONT
C.on in 2 × 2 rib 58 (62, 66, 70,
74) sts.
RC 000, T2/2, K 30 rs.
Trans sts to M/bed.
RC 000, MT, K 50 rs.
*For pocket, K cent 30 sts onto
nylon cord.
Leave sts in WP*. K 50 rs.
Rep from * to *.
Cont to K until RC 154.

Shape front & armhole
C.off 10 sts beg next r. K 1 r.
Dec 1 st FF at left next & ev foll
3rd rs until 21 (25, 29, 33, 37) sts
rem.
Cont to K until RC 244.
C.off rem sts.

LEFT FRONT
K as for right front rev all shaping

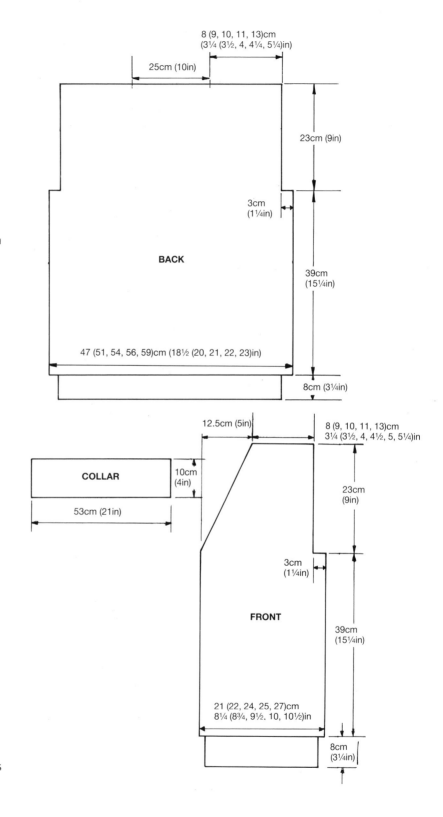

8 (9, 10, 11, 13)cm
(3¼ (3½, 4, 4¼, 5¼)in)

25cm (10in)

23cm (9in)

3cm
(1¼in)

BACK

39cm
(15¼in)

47 (51, 54, 56, 59)cm (18½ (20, 21, 22, 23)in)

8cm (3¼in)

12.5cm (5in)

8 (9, 10, 11, 13)cm
3¼ (3½, 4, 4½, 5, 5¼)in

COLLAR

10cm
(4in)

23cm
(9in)

53cm (21in)

3cm
(1¼in)

FRONT

39cm
(15¼in)

21 (22, 24, 25, 27)cm
8¼ (8¾, 9½, 10, 10½)in

8cm
(3¼in)

SLEEVES

C.on in 2 × 2 rib 76 sts.
RC 000, T2/2, K 30 rs.
Trans sts to M/bed.
RC 000, MT.
Inc 1 st both ends ev foll 4th r
until 158 sts.
Cont to K until RC 170 (170, 170,
180, 180).
Trans sts to 2 × 2 rib.
T3/3, K 20 rs.
C.off loosely.

BANDS

C.on in 2 × 2 rib 24 sts.
RC 000, T2/2, K 6 rs.
*Work buttonhole over ns 15 &
16 – K 24 rs *.
Rep 6 more times.
Cont to K until RC 750.
Check band is long enough.
C.off.

COLLAR

C.on in 2 × 2 rib 150 sts.
RC 000, T3/3, K 30 rs.
C.off.

POCKET TOPS

(K four)
C.on in 2 × 2 rib 30 sts.
RC 000, T4/4, K 10 rs.
Trans sts to M/bed.
MT, K 1 r.
With wrong side facing pick up
30 sts from below nylon cord.
K 1 r.
C.off.
DO NOT REMOVE NYLON
CORD

POCKET LINING

(K four)
Bring forward 31 ns.
With wrong side facing and with
work upside down pick up 31 sts
from other side of nylon cord.
MT, K 30 rs.
C.off.

TO MAKE UP

Block & steam press.
Join shoulder seams.
Insert sleeves, join side & sleeve
seams.
Sew band to front.
Backstitch collar to band & slip st
down at front.
Stitch pocket tops to fronts.
Sew pocket linings to inside.
Sew buttons to front.
Press.

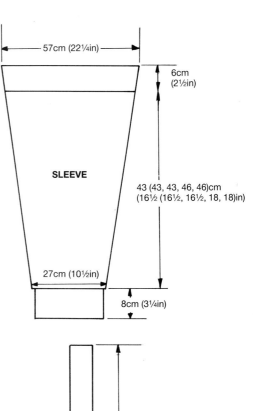

57cm (22¼in)

6cm (2½in)

SLEEVE

43 (43, 43, 46, 46)cm
(16½ (16½, 16½, 18, 18)in)

27cm (10½in)

8cm (3¼in)

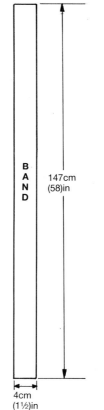

BAND

147cm (58)in

4cm (1½)in

Cardigan—see pattern on page 123

Motor bike sweater.

(See photograph on page 117)

Sizes 91 (97, 102, 107)cm (36 (38, 40, 42)in)

Materials 1 (1, 2, 2) cones BK Superwash 4-ply
Small amount col B
Chart for electronic machs or work manual selection

Tension 32 sts × 40 rs = 10cm (4in)
T at approx 6.

BACK

Col A, c.on in 1 × 1 rib 151 (159, 167, 175) sts.
RC 000, T1/1, K 30 rs.
Trans sts to M/bed.
RC 000, MT, K 150 (156, 160, 166) rs.

Shape Armholes
C.off 10 (13, 13, 13) sts beg next 2 rs.
Cont to K until RC 246 (260, 272, 286).

Shape Shoulders
C.off 35 (38, 38, 41) sts beg next 2 rs.
Rel work on WY.

FRONT

Col A, c.on in 1 × 1 rib 151 (159, 167, 175) sts.
RC 000, T1/1, K 30 rs.
Trans sts to M/bed.
RC 000, MT, K 86 (92, 96, 102) rs.
Set Electronic machines or work in manual selection from chart
At Same Time
Cont to work in patt until RC 150 (156, 160, 166).

Shape Armholes
Cont in patt **At Same Time**
C.off 10 (13, 13, 13) sts beg next 2 rs.

Cont to work in patt until RC 179 (185, 189, 195).
Break off col B.
Cont to K until RC 206 (220, 232, 246).

Shape Neck
Push cent 17 (19, 21, 23) sts into HP.
K all sts at left back onto nylon cord.
Work on right side only.

Always taking yarn round last ns in HP.
At oppos end to carr push 6 sts into HP. K 2 rs.
Push 4 sts into HP. K 2 rs.
Push 2 sts into HP next & foll alt rs 5 times in all.
Dec 1 st at neck next & foll alt rs until 35 (38, 38, 41) sts rem.
Cont to K until RC 246 (260, 272, 286).
C.off rem sts.

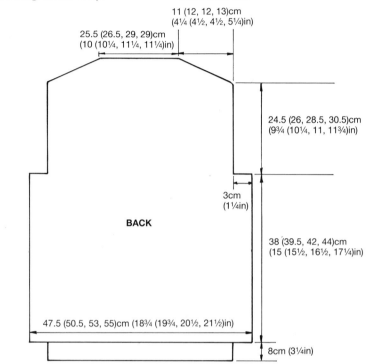

11 (12, 12, 13)cm (4¼ (4½, 4½, 5¼)in)

25.5 (26.5, 29, 29)cm (10 (10¼, 11¼, 11¼)in)

24.5 (26, 28.5, 30.5)cm (9¾ (10¼, 11, 11¾)in)

3cm (1¼in)

BACK

38 (39.5, 42, 44)cm (15 (15½, 16½, 17¼)in)

47.5 (50.5, 53, 55)cm (18¾ (19¾, 20½, 21½)in)

8cm (3¼in)

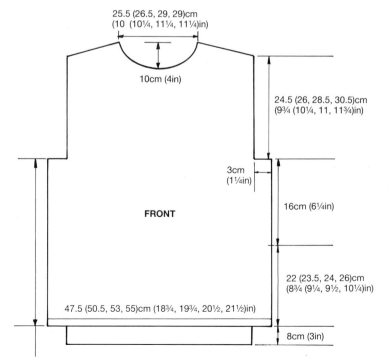

25.5 (26.5, 29, 29)cm (10 (10¼, 11¼, 11¼)in)

10cm (4in)

24.5 (26, 28.5, 30.5)cm (9¾ (10¼, 11, 11¾)in)

3cm (1¼in)

16cm (6¼in)

FRONT

22 (23.5, 24, 26)cm (8¾ (9¼, 9½, 10¼)in)

47.5 (50.5, 53, 55)cm (18¾ (19¾, 20½, 21½)in)

8cm (3in)

38 (39.5, 42, 44)cm (15 (15½, 16½, 17¼)in)

K left side to match rev all shaping.
Rel sts in HP on WY.

SLEEVES
Col A, c.on in 1 × 1 rib 67 (71, 75, 79) sts.
RC 000, T1/1, K 30 rs.
Trans sts to M/bed. Inc 1 st.
RC 000, MT, K 4 rs.
Inc 1 st both ends next & foll 4th rs until 142 (152, 162, 172) sts.
Cont to K until RC 180 (190, 190, 200) rs.
C.off loosely.

NECKBAND
Join left shoulder seam.
Col A, c.on in 1 × 1 rib 163 (167, 177, 181) sts.
RC 000, T5/5, K 4 rs. T4/4, K 4 rs. T3/3, K 4 rs. T2/2, K 8 rs. T3/3, K 4 rs. T4/4, K 4 rs. T5/5, K 4 rs.
With wrong side facing pick up sts held on WY from front and back neck.
MT, K 1 r. T10, K 1 r.
C.off with latch tool.

TO MAKE UP
Join right shoulder.
Inset sleeves.
Sew side & sleeve seams. Fold neckband to inside & slip st into pos.
Using silver thread Swiss darn Z flash on motor bike tank.

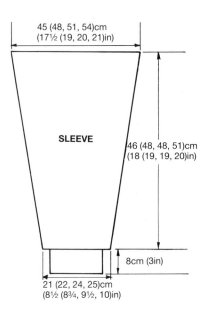

SLEEVE

45 (48, 51, 54)cm (17½, 19, 20, 21)in)

46 (48, 48, 51)cm (18 (19, 19, 20)in)

8cm (3in)

21 (22, 24, 25)cm (8½, 8¾, 9½, 10)in)

POSTSCRIPT

As a dedicated hand knitter, making up my own patterns, my first encounter with a knitting machine 15 years ago was not exactly a case of love at first sight, all those wires and thingumajigs certainly put me off. Being fascinated by knitting I had to have a go, and like most new machine knitters I wanted to run before I could walk.

The first garments I knitted were a six panelled skirt with a fairisle top. I literally drove a friend to distraction with all my cries for help, but by the end of the week I was proudly wearing my new suit and was hooked on machine knitting.

I now wanted to understand the machine and to learn how to use it properly so I set about working through the instruction book. The more I used the machine the more fascinated I became, the possibilities it offered for patterning seemed endless but as a beginner, wanting to practice all the basic techniques I had difficulty finding simple classic patterns, so I set about making up my own resulting in a collection of patterns being published. Since that time I have designed and written patterns for other magazines and have edited an English version of an American knitting machine pattern book. I now spend all my time designing and writing patterns for knitting machines.

After all these years, machine knitting still intrigues me and I'm pleased to say I enjoy every minute I spend working on machines. I'm delighted to see more knitting machines are being sold than ever before and machine knitting continues to be one of the fastest growing leisure/hobby industries in Britain today.

I have been extremely lucky, my interest in knitting machines has taken me to America, Thailand and Japan where I was fortunate enough to visit Jones & Brother knitting machine schools. I have run knitting clubs and taught machine knitting. This has left me little time for my other hobbies which include oil painting, sketching, reading, tapestry, and embroidery. When I do have time to spare, I either listen to music or expend physical energy working out at my local gym or dancing.

Anyone who takes on the task of writing a book needs help and I'm no exception. I would like to thank Sue, whose typing ability is 100% better than my own, and to Jill and Eileen for their tireless efforts. Working on any project with a deadline to meet, creates pressures; working on a knitting pattern book where it is of the utmost importance to have each pattern checked, the worst possible thing that can happen is to have not one, but both my treasured 'check knitters' off sick. Eileen in hospital and Jill with a sprained ankle and 'knitting hand', but because they are who they are they have both come through with flying colours and have patiently checked every pattern. Eileen's husband is now intrigued by knitting machines – for him I think it's been a case of 'If you can't beat them – join them'. He is now knitting his own knitwear.

My thanks must also go to Iris Bishop who contributed the Woven Fringed Top suit. Iris has built up a considerable reputation for unique and exciting ideas in the machine knitting world and specialises in 'fabric' designs and techniques. Her range of publications includes designs for Fair Isle, lace, braids and edgings, lettering etc. and a fascinating design kit using 'fabric dye pastels' to add extra colour to Fair Isle knitting.